Parade Ring Edge

A Punter's Guide to Assessing Pre-Race Fitness and Behaviour in Racehorses

Copyright © Stephen Lang 2025

All rights reserved

No part of this book may be reproduced, stored in a retrieval system, or transmitted in any form or by any means, electronic, mechanical, photocopying, recording, or otherwise, without the prior written permission of the author, except for the use of brief quotations in a review as allowed under the Copyright Act. The author asserts his moral rights to the work and its contents.

Disclaimer: While every effort has been made to ensure the accuracy of the information presented in this book, the author makes no representations or warranties regarding the completeness, reliability or suitability of the content. The material is intended for informational purposes only, and any reliance the reader places on the information is strictly at the reader's risk. The author shall not be liable for any loss, injury or damage, whether direct or indirect, arising from the use or misuse of the information contained herein, including but not limited to any errors or omissions.

Web: paraderingedge.com

ISBN: 978-0-646-72222-1

GAMBLE RESPONSIBLY: IF GAMBLING BECOMES A PROBLEM READERS ARE ENCOURAGED TO SEEK PROFESSIONAL HELP.

Acknowledgements

In Memory of – **Brian Lang**
Gerard Lang

Many thanks to those I have confided in and who've given helpful feedback and support –

Ron Budd
Neil Grieve
Drew Patchell
David Frolley
Michelle O'Brien
Joe Errante
Peter Anthonisz
Jack Lang
Patrick Lang

Enquiries re Business, Project Management, Yard Information etc

paraderingedge@gmail.com

Website

paraderingedge.com

Contents

Chapter 1. Horse Watching and Horse Watchers 1
Chapter 2. Book Notes 3
    Aims and Content 3
    Data and Metrics 4
    The Variable Descriptions 5
Chapter 3. Factors of the Head 6
    Facial Expressions 7
    Ears Pricked 9
    Ears Negative 9
    Bit Play 10
    Bit Grinding 10
    Salivate Mild 11
    Salivate Heavy 11
    Still Mouth 11
    Head Toss 12
Chapter 4. Factors of the Neck and Shoulder 13
    Neck Positive 13
    Neck Negative 14
    Neck Arched 14
    Neck Twisted 15
    Neck Horizontal 15
    Ground Licker 15
    The Average Neck 16
    Shoulder Positive 16
Chapter 5. Factors of the Mid-Section 18
    Rib Cage Positive 18
    Rib Cage Negative 19
    Tension Line 19
    Underbelly Negative 19
    Flanks Negative 20
Chapter 6. Factors of the Rear End 21
    Money Mark Positive 21
    Money Mark Negative 21
    Racing Dimple Positive 22
    Racing Dimple Negative 22
    Rump Top Negative 22
    Hip Pointing 23
    Thigh Negative 24
    Rump Top Positive 24
    The Average Rear End 25
    Tail Swishing 25
    Tail Jammed 26
Chapter 7. Putting It All Together-Whole Body Fitness Grading 27
    Fit 27
    Average 28
    Fat 29
    Thin 29
Chapter 8. Walking Styles 36
    Power Walk 36

Walking Short	37
Jig Jogging	37
Double Tracking	38
Scuffing	38
Miscellaneous	38
Chapter 9. Behaviour	**40**
Focus/Transition	40
Behaviour Negative	41
Chapter 10. Coat	**44**
Glowing Coat	44
Dappled Coat	44
Dull Coat	45
Chapter 11. Sweating	**46**
Bum Sweat	46
Body Sweat	46
Chapter 12. Size	**49**
Big	49
Small	49
Chapter 13. Droppings	**50**
Loose	50
Firm	51
Chapter 14. Grooms	**52**
Groom Negative	52
Chapter 15. Canter Off	**54**
Canter Off Positive	54
Canter Off Negative	55
Chapter 16. Behind The Gates	**57**
Chapter 17. Post Race	**58**
Chapter 18. Stalls	**59**
Chapter 19. Bandages	**60**
Chapter 20. Spurs	**61**
Chart 1 - Factor Groupings	**62**
Chapter 21. Factor Discussion, Tables and Combinations	**63**
Factor Groupings	63
Table 1 - Overall Factor Impact Values	64
Distance Effects	66
Table 2 - Factor Impact Values by Distance	66
Table 3 - Factors with Increased or Maintained Positivity-Short to Long Distance	68
Table 4 – Factors that Increase in Negativity – Short to Long Distance	69
Market Influences	70
Table 5 – Market Influence on Impact Values	70
Combinations	72
Table 6 – Fit (32) Combinations	72
Table 7 – Average (33) Combinations	74
Table 8 – Fat (34) Combinations	75
Table 9 – Thin (35) Combinations	76
Observing Factor Changes	77
Factor Profiling	78
Age and Stage of Training Preparation	79
Trainer Styles	80
Wet Tracks	81

Chapter 22. Actual v Expected – The A/E Index 83
- A/E Description 83
  - Table 10 – A/E Index Values 84
  - Table 11 – Impact Value and A/E Comparison of Top 5 Variables 85
- Factor Combinations and the A/E Index 86
  - Table 12 – A/E Index Values of Fit and Positive Variables 86
  - Table 13 – A/E Index Values of Fit and Negative Variables 87
  - Table 14 – A/E Index Values of Average and Positive Variables 87
  - Table 15 – A/E Index Values of Average and Negative Variables 88
- Distance and the A/E Index 88
  - Table 16 – A/E Index Values of Short, Mid, Long Distances 88
- A/E Index Summary 92

Chapter 23. "At The Parade" 93
- Access and Positioning 93
- Viewing Procedure 93
- Mind Games 94

Chapter 24. "Parade Transcripts" 96
- Parade (1) 96
- Parade (2) 99

Chapter 25. "From Yard to Race" 103
- Table 17 – From Yard to Race Variables 103

Chapter 26. "From The TV" 106

Chapter 27. "In Running" Horse Watching Thoughts 109
- Table 18 – "In Running" Variables 110

Chapter 28. Applying The Knowledge – Data Usage 112
- Basic Usage 112
- Ratings 112
- Machine Learning - Artificial Intelligence (AI) 113
- My Data Usage Journey 113

Chapter 29. "Final Thoughts" 115
- "My Journey" 116

Chapter 1. Horse Watching and Horse Watchers

Horse Watching – "The pre-race evaluation of a racehorse's fitness, walking style, demeanour and behaviour, within the prevailing environmental conditions."

Also known as – paddock assessment, physicality handicapping, equine appraising, yard watching, mounting yard inspection and many more.

And those that practice it – horse watchers, yardies, paddock assessors, among many titles, including the job title I was given as a professional horse watcher, "Equine Condition Analyst".

And where it takes place – mounting yard, paddock enclosure, parade ring, bird cage, saddling enclosure and saddling paddock.

The terminology can vary regionally, but general usage in this book will be, horse watching for the activity, horse watcher for those who practice it and mounting yard for the location of it.

In recent years in Australia, where I am based, horse watching has experienced a strong surge in popularity. It has evolved from a small number of watchers passing information back to bookmakers and major punters at the metropolitan meetings for a few dollars, to analysts in attendance at most meetings funnelling back yard information through the media, major corporate bookmaking operations, paid services and large syndicates.

There appears to have been a huge awakening among these players that the race day fitness and disposition of a racehorse may actually have a bearing on their performance, which in turn creates an opportunity of obtaining an all-important wagering edge for them. Having worked as a professional yard analyst for just under twenty years, attending three to six meetings a week and assessing thousands of horses in that time, I can safely say that the information gleaned about a horse from the yard, unequivocally has a bearing on correctly predicting what the performance may be. Both positive and negative performance.

For me there is no doubt that the contribution of yard analysis to the complete picture of race prediction, rivals the importance of any of the well accepted factors such as, class, weight, time and speed mapping. All those can be nullified by a horse with a poor yard assessment.

So, what are the skills required for someone to become proficient in assessing the pre-race condition of a racehorse? The first thing to make blatantly clear is that there is no magical "horse whispering" gift necessary. Most people would be blessed with enough ability to do well at it. Secondly, I don't believe horse handling experience is a prerequisite either. Those that I've helped that hadn't worked with horses often had an advantage as they had no preconceived opinions of what were good or bad variables.

Probably, the best ingredients needed for horse watching are simply, a keen interest, a bit of plain common sense and good observation skills with the ability to identify subtle cues. These attributes are pretty much the recipe for success at most things and are the foundation for proficiency in learning, understanding and identifying horse watching variables.

The hardest thing for many horse watchers to do is to separate what they see in the yard, from what they know about the horse's form. It's a conflict of what the brain already knows (the horse's form), what the eyes are seeing (the horse's physical and mental state) and what the ears are hearing (a media presenter's thoughts, punters comments and other distractions).

It's human nature to be deflated after you've spent hours studying the form or paid for a rating service and come up with a best bet only to see it at the yard, trained right off with muscle depletion, sweating, head

Chapter 1. Horse Watching and Horse Watchers

tossing and unruly. It couldn't be yelling at you any louder that today wasn't the day, but one's ability to convince themselves that "it's not that bad" is often the overriding emotion, when deep down you know that the proper thing to do is to forego the bet.

Like most, I have succumbed to this in the past, but when working as a paddock analyst for syndicates and professional punters I quickly realised they wanted their data pure, not tainted by someone's form opinions. My personal method of avoiding the influences that knowing form or listening to pundits might bring was to not know it and not listen to it. I wouldn't know who was in the field until they entered the mounting yard and avoided knowing their names, reducing them to saddlecloth numbers.

Going to that extreme isn't necessary for those wanting to include yard watching in their race prediction analysis, but it is a reminder to separate the form and yard when actually doing the yard watching and work out the balance of the two on completion.

Usually, the most difficult decision the beginner analyst will encounter is the classification of fitness grades. There are four of these, Fit, Average, Fat and Thin and there are 16 physical structures used to evaluate which fitness brackets a horse qualifies for. Chart 1 – Factor Groupings shows how the flow of variables works in achieving a final assessment.

As would be expected, practice and experience are the keys to developing one's skill to a level where a passing glance is sufficient to quickly determine a horse's fitness grading. Even though confidence may be lacking in nominating fitness categories initially, I believe the first time at the track, after learning and familiarising oneself with the factor descriptions, should enable some reasonable decisions to be made based on some physical characteristics, walks and behavioural identifications.

Fitness gradings don't necessarily have to follow the pattern exhibited in this book. As one develops the skills to identify all the variables described, they may also develop a preference for a certain style of horse or profile. Be that from a type of walk, muscle structure or behavioural pattern. The more you watch parades the more these distinct styles or profiles become recognisable to you.

Chapter 2. Book Notes

Many punters would have spent their whole betting lives never bothering to learn how to view a horse's condition or even attend a mounting yard parade. Having spent years on the flip side of that scenario I can only wonder about the difference it may have made if they'd taken the time to learn a little and attend the parade ring to ensure their selection was profiling acceptably for the race.

It's not the daunting task some people assume and there's no need to have any horse knowledge. If you can pick which end is the head and which end is the tail, you shouldn't have a problem following the descriptions of the factors. With practical experience and an understanding of the variables described here, one should be able to progress from basically zero horse knowledge to being capable of extracting a reasonable fitness and demeanour assessment from a pre-race parade, fairly quickly.

The use of technical and physiological names and terms are intentionally avoided as much as possible, as the information is provided for the uptake of the average punter who's more likely to be a non-horse person. Also, you won't come across terms such as "offset knees", "turned out in front", "upright pasterns" and the like. They are phrases used in horse conformational assessments and are for people to judge at yearling sales and purchase inspections. The appraisals made here are concerned with a horse's acquisition from its training and racing program, such as fitness, muscle development and behavioural outlook.

Each chapter that contains descriptions of variables ends with an "At the Yard Checklist" section. It is a list of questions relevant to the topic that the watcher should ask of each horse, or the horse they are interested in, when doing a yard inspection. It serves as a quick reference rundown of the chapter's factors.

Aims and Content

The following is a walkthrough of the content contained in the ensuing chapters and the intentions of how the information is conveyed.

- Firstly, the main aim was to provide the information in an easily readable and understandable format, suitable for the non-horse person, punter, racegoer, horse lover or anyone interested in the subject.

- Assemble a group of variables that are commonly seen at pre-race parades and are within the reach of people to identify comfortably. The result was 54 factors that cover muscle definitions, fitness categories, walking styles, behaviours and more.

- Provide descriptions of the factors that clearly show how to identify each one. This has been achieved with the inclusion of pictures with diagrams where applicable.

- Convey practical applications of doing a pre-race assessment. The "At the Parade" chapter discusses this, and the "Parade Transcripts" chapter offers, comments with pictures, of two races that I assessed.

- Provide validity of the variables via the use of backing data.

- Use metrics to show values of the factors, so they can be quantified and compared with each other to ascertain relative importance. The choice here was Impact Values (IV) and the Actual/Expected Index (A/E).

- Explore what racing factors may influence change in the IV and A/E values. This is covered by examining the influences of race distance, market position and variables in combination.

- Examine if there is any carry over in traits seen in the yard to race behaviours. The "From Yard to

Race" chapter looks at correlations between variables exhibited in the yard with the frequency of some common in-race idiosyncrasies.

- The "From the TV" chapter looks at the vagaries of assessing horses off media vision feeds, providing a possible alternative to racecourse attendance.

- Is horse watching possible during a race? This is explored assessing a group of variables over 800 races.

- How can the data from yard assessing be used? The Data Usage section offers some suggestions from basic applications, to formulating ratings and odds to even the more advanced methods of Machine Learning and Artificial Intelligence.

Data and Metrics

Collection of the data was made over a period of four years, by me, from assessments made at race meetings, with the assistance of fixed and 360-degree cameras for reviewing and from televised mounting yard parades. The meetings covered the full gamut of class types that we have here in Australia, from the group races of the metropolitan races down to the maidens of the lower-level bush meetings. So virtually every type and quality of racehorse would've been encountered and assessed along the way.

When doing the appraisals and collecting the data there are a few requirements that I always adhere to. Firstly, the variable must be consistently displayed for most of the horse's parade time. It may be intermittent, such as bouts of head tossing or jig jogging, but those bouts must continue to occur during the parade. Secondly, I always give a horse some time to settle down after it first enters the parade. Often a horse may jig jog into the new environment, but before marking it as a jig jogger, some slack should be given, maybe half a lap or so, to see if it stops doing it, as many certainly will. Also, all my assessments were done prior to the jockeys mounting, with the exception being the Canter Off factors, as they obviously occur with the rider mounted and out on the track.

The factor descriptions don't delve into the cause, they concentrate on explaining how to identify them. We can't always account for why horses display different attributes and in horse watching we must collect the data and respect the results. There are a lot of conflicting opinions among horse watchers about how horses should look, what's positive or negative, but my belief is that the data will tell me what is real and that is the process adopted in this book. None of the values depicted are my opinion, they are what the data I've collected says. Having said that, the positivity or negativity of the variables do fall the way most horse people would expect, with the data providing confirmation and an indication of the strength or importance of what is being witnessed.

Two similar metrics are used for the evaluation of the data collected on each variable. They are the Impact Value (IV) and the Actual/Expected Index (A/E Index). The Impact Value figure is used throughout the variable description sections and the A/E Index has a whole chapter dedicated to it further on.

The IV is an easy figure to understand as it tells us whether the variable is winning its fair share of races. Its simplicity is in the fact it revolves around the figure 1, where anything above 1 means the factor is winning more than expected for its occurrence in the population and hence a positive factor, with a negative factor declared for anything under 1. A figure of 1 means the variable is returning the normal number of winners expected from its occurrence in the population.

The calculation is –

(winners with variable / all winners) / (runners with variable / all runners)

As an example, the Head Toss factor is a negative, returning an IV of 0.78 and the Power Walk returns a

Chapter 2. Book Notes

very positive 1.87 IV, whereas the Salivate Heavy variable returns 1.02 and would have to be considered normal for the population. The IV is an easily referenced metric that powerfully describes the value of a factor and enables comparisons across all the variables.

The other metric used is the odds. These are all "real time" odds, not Betfair Starting Price, as they were all sourced from the Betfair Exchange around 2 minutes before the jump, as the horses were circling behind the starting gates.

The Variable Descriptions

These begin in the next Chapter (3) and continue through to Chapter (20). They work in order from head to tail, then overall fitness, followed by walking styles, behaviours, coats, sweats, size, droppings, grooms, canter offs and 5 sundry items.

Each of the 54 variables is given a reference number, along with its Impact Value and these are located beneath the headings.

The advice is to firstly have a study of Chart 1 to understand how they are grouped and to take some time reading and rereading each description to obtain a solid understanding of how to identify them when you attend a parade. 54 variables to identify may at first seem a bit overwhelming, but don't be perturbed, all the people I've dealt with haven't encountered any difficulty doing their yard assessments after getting familiar with the factors. Yard watching doesn't come down to having to check 54 factors on each horse as they pass by in the parade. Once you know them all, the ones that you have to mark will stand out to you.

Chapter 3. Factors of the Head

Close observations of features of the equine head can prove a valuable insight into assessing a horse's mental and physical condition prior to a race, which in turn can tell us how focused, distracted or apprehensive they're feeling about what they are about to confront. Make no mistake, they know what is coming.

Facial features can depict negative and positive signs, some are subtle and are often overlooked by yard analysts while some are glaringly obvious. With practice and proper identification one can really begin to predict almost what the horse is thinking. I'm sure most of us have heard comments from trainers and experienced horse people about "getting inside the horse's head", so as parade ring watchers this is our opportunity to "get inside their heads". Definitely an invaluable asset in assessing their race day disposition.

Physical features of the head that are used for factor assessment here are,

- Mouth
- Nostrils
- Chewing Muscles
- Eyes
- Ears

The majority of the variables described are negatives with one of the positives among the most important factors in horse watching you can identify – Still Mouth.

As with most factors in the pre-race parade the horse needs to constantly display the factor to validate its presence. It's quite normal for horses to occasionally put their ears back, chew on the bit or open their mouth and so on in the parade but this doesn't equate to being assessed as a bit chewer etc. Determination of the factor is by the frequency of it. You must be satisfied that the horse is clearly and consistently showing the trait.

One important factor when looking at variables of the head is the effect of headgear. Both in gear changes and in first time applications. Most jurisdictions provide gear notifications lists, something watchers should arm themselves with. It is an advantage to be able to assess how the horse is accepting changes of gear or new gear.

In my area every race generally has horses with gear notifications. Tongue ties, bit changes, blinkers, winkers, pacifiers, cross over nose bands etc. Reactions can range from complete acceptance to severe head tossing and discomfort. It is a must for anyone investing to get to the parade ring and have the knowledge to be able to assess the horse's comfort or discomfort with gear adjustments.

Negative reactions to gear changes can cause a carryover into the tractability of a horse during a race. Parade ring factors and their effect on racing are further discussed in Chapter 25

An important consideration when assessing head factors is observing the head both when in hand and after mounting. Look for changes in intensity of a factor between the two. Has what you thought was borderline for being marked prior to being mounted become obvious and intensified or has it disappeared? Or has a factor appeared when ridden that was previously not noticeable? The important thing to notice is change. The expressions of the head can often tell us if the horse is accepting or resentful of being ridden. The signs can be subtle, such as tension in the nose area causing wrinkling to the obvious like severe head tossing.

Prior to delving into the descriptions of the head factors, which are predominately negative, let's break down the components of what a horse displaying 'head comfort" looks like.

Chapter 3. Factors of the Head

 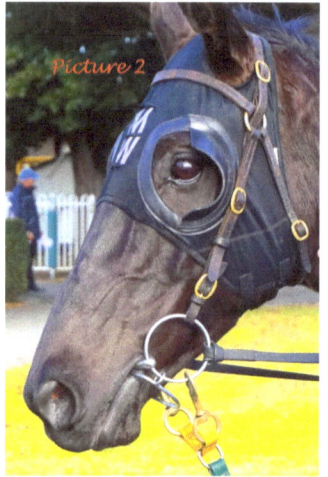 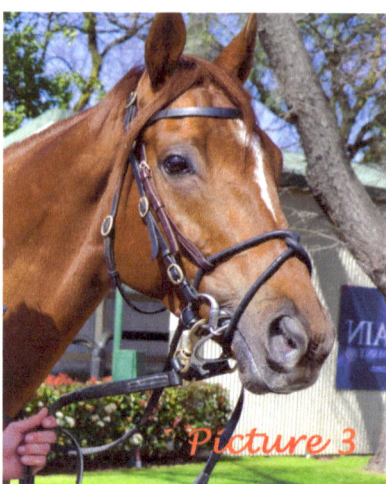

Pictures 1, 2 and 3 all depict horses showing a good degree of comfort whilst also fitted with varying items of headgear. Picture 1 a cross over nose band, 2 blinkers and ring bit and 3 with a ring bit and cross over. None of them are showing signs of discomfort from the gear.

So how can we reasonably assume they are "head comfortable"?

Firstly, the head carriage is set at around 45 degrees to the ground in all pictures, there's no elevation, sideways turn or head tossing going on.

Looking at the ears they are forward in an alert position attentive and tuned in to where they're heading and the surroundings.

The eyes all look sharp with no white displayed and with no obvious creasing above the eye in the brow area and the chewing muscles area on the sides look relaxed.

All look very comfortable in the nostrils with the outsides nice and rounded and 3 showing no sign of tension with wrinkling between the nostrils.

Mouths are all closed with the lips sitting comfortably against each other. No pulling back of the lips exposing the teeth.

These are the signs you're looking for when assessing comfort of the horse's head. Generally, with these horses there is no forward resistance, they know what's going on, they're at ease with it and are willing with an accommodating attitude. They may raise their head to observe something, turn their ears back to be attentive behind, chew on the bit or open their mouth and so on but only occasionally and that's normal. It should be the first question the yard analyst asks on initial observation of a horse in the parade ring, how is this horse presenting in the head today? They usually tell you and it's not hard to identify.

Let's now work through descriptions of the variables so one can learn to identify them.

Facial Expressions

Ref: Var.1   Impact Value   0.74

The values for this factor were derived from observations of multiple facial features. The mouth, nostrils,

Chapter 3. Factors of the Head

chewing muscles and eyes. Only one of the feature's traits had to be on display for it to be marked although quite often horses presented with two or three traits.

Criteria for marking was it had to be obvious and as all assessments it had to be consistent.

Picture 4 depicts quite a few traits that would prompt the marking of this category. The picture is a good example and was shot due to the horse constantly displaying the features as it paraded around the mounting yard.

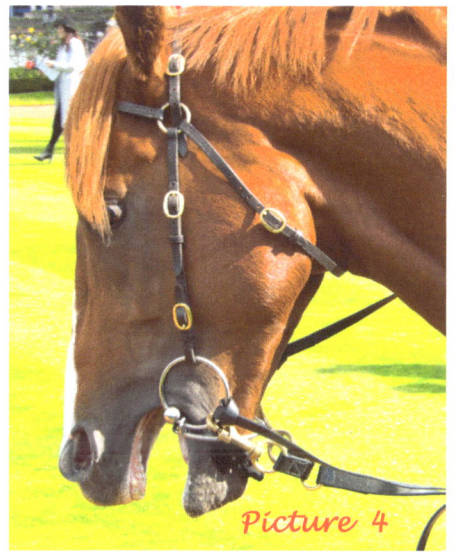

First thing to notice is the obvious open mouth. It's not a normal position to maintain, as this horse did. Visible below the bit is the black stocking material used for a tongue tie. The open mouth may be caused by resentment to the tongue tie. There is clearly a degree of discomfort going on in the mouth.

There is slight pull back of the upper lip causing partial exposure of the teeth and in turn you can see that the nostrils are beginning to lose that nice relaxed rounded shape (Picture 1) and taking on a more elongated appearance with the upper rim beginning to come to a point or upside-down v shape.

From the upper edge of the nostril through to the eye there is a lot of tightening of the muscles. The eye is also showing a lot of white. In horses this can be a sign of fear, pain, apprehension or discomfort. Compare the head to Picture 1, a vast difference.

In Picture 5 there are multiple examples of head discomfort. The upper lip is raised with the teeth and gums fully exposed, the muzzle area scrunched causing the nostrils to distort and the chewing muscles area is very tight. The grey area above the nostrils is where nasal strips have been applied to help with the animals breathing.

This is why it's imperative that the horse watcher take note of gear changes, as it's a possibility this might be a first-time application of the strips, and they are the cause of the negative facial expressions.

In Picture 6 there is a lot of tension in the upper lip with the nostrils losing their rounded shape and vertical wrinkles forming between the nostrils.

The eyes of the horse should be bright with a deep rich colour (Picture 1) with no white visible and no partial closure of the upper lid.

The muscles above the eyes should be relaxed and free of any creasing or wrinkling that may be caused by stress or tension. I have found this is more easily noticed if the horse is able to be viewed in the stalls or tie ups compared to when it is being led around the mounting yard. The upper rim of the eye becomes angular and the skin above it on the brow follows the contour in creases. It's a tense frowned look and you can sense that the horse is concerned about something.

Chapter 3. Factors of the Head

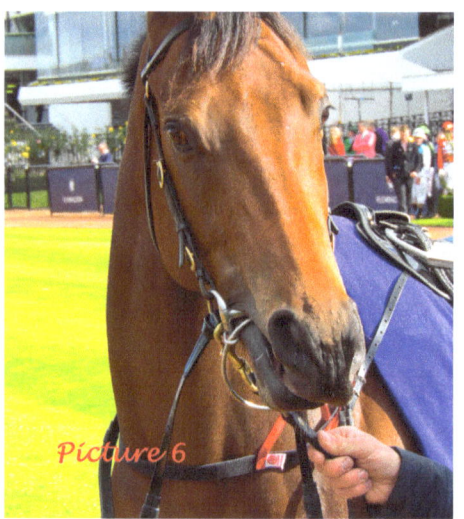

Picture 6

Facial expressions are important to be able to identify as they have a negative Impact Value figure and a very low Win%. They are a window to how horses are feeling about what is facing them. They can be subtle too. I've seen horses that parade with slightly worse muzzle tension than the example in Picture 6 with no other negative signs at all and probably appearing relaxed to most observers, yet they perform below expectations. High probability the horse was feeling something, and this was its method of showing it.

Facial expressions won't be the most prolific factors that get observed and they are often apparent in tandem with other head factors such as tossing, bit chewing and negative ear shape.

In summary, we are using physical features of the equine head and observing reshaping of those features to determine the animal's demeanour and the acceptance of any gear applied. Open mouth, tense wrinkled upper lip, elongated nostrils, tight chewing muscles down the side of the head, white eye, lazy partially closed eyelid, creasing above eye. These all depict shape change from the previously described head comfortable horse.

Ears Pricked

Ref: Var.2   Impact Value 1.38

Supported by a healthy Impact Value, Pricked Ears are a very positive attribute when displayed by the equine athlete.

Picture 7

The ears are positioned upright and forward as in Picture 7 and in Picture 1. They may turn rearwards as the horse tunes in to something behind, but should always return to the forward, pricked position.

This factor represents a horse that is alert, sensibly sensitive to his surroundings, comfortable moving forward, focused into the environment and the occasion and most importantly and likely, pain free.

They move through a parade conscious of everything but not reactive, maintaining the pricked ears as their primary position. They convey a physical and mental sense of authority and contentment. This is definitely not a factor telling us they'd rather be elsewhere.

Ears Negative

Ref: Var.3   Impact Value 0.6

In this category we have the opposite of pricked ears with the Impact Value supporting a very negative factor. Negative ears are assessed by identifying three ear positions.

Firstly, there is the flat back or pinned ears position. The ears lay hard back against the neck top with the tips pointing towards the rear. It is an aggressive position and a sign of anger and strong annoyance. You're probably more likely to see this in the stalls area when saddling up or getting groomed. In the mounting yard a horse may pin them back at another horse briefly as a sign of dominance, but it is not something that was regularly observed. I tended to look for it when the rider was about to be legged up.

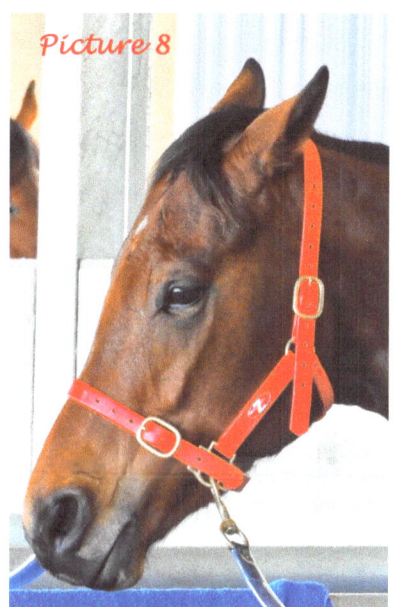

In Picture 8 we have the sideways ears. They hang out to the side, can be slightly back, the area between them appears wider and there is not forward or backward attentive movement. They just don't appear to be registering anything. This position can be representative of lethargy, disinterest, possible soreness and a general lack of enthusiasm for racing. Presentation is often accompanied with a walk that lacks forward purpose or has rear end hoof scuffing. Twitching ears flick back and forward sharply and continuously. The horse gives off a nervous disposition, is sensitive to everything around it and the ears flicker in response. It's normal for the ears to turn rearward when the horse is attentive to something behind but it's in a controlled manner and not in a nervous twitching manner. Implications of this trait are that the horse is showing concern, nerves and lacking concentration. It's often associated with "flighty" behaviour and not the preferred headspace prior to performance.

Bit Play

Ref: Var.4   Impact Value 1.06

This is where a horse chews on or plays with the bit in their mouth. It's clearly visible to see them chomping away and also audible via the jangling sound made.

The Impact Value implies that Bit Play returns close to a normal win rate compared to its occurrence in the population. It is very prevalent and a high percentage of horses in each race do it. This most likely contributes to a watering down effect on the Impact Value.

There are degrees of it with some horses doing it more aggressively than others and, in these cases, they are often observed displaying associated factors such as drooling saliva and head tossing.

It can be a normal habit for a lot of horses and if records are kept it can provide an opportunity to identify a change of habit which is so important with traits and behaviours.

Bit Grinding

Ref: Var.5   Impact Value .83

This is an audible sound caused by pressure from the horse's upper and lower teeth being forced against each other creating a grinding noise. Their mouth is usually closed and muscles around the jaw and side of the head appear tight. There aren't always other factors displayed in conjunction with grinding and a lot of those exhibiting it tend to walk the yard just fully concentrated on their grinding.

It's not one of the most frequent variables a yard watcher will come across and it may be a bad habit of the horse or indicative of tension.

Salivate Mild

Ref: Var.6   Impact Value   1.13

Picture 9 is a good example of a Mild Salivate at the higher end of the scale before it tips over into the Heavy Salivate category. It presents as a lipstick style covering of saliva over the lips and can range from a thin film to a thicker load as in the picture. Carries a slightly positive impact value.

Mild drooling is differentiated from heavy drooling by it not reaching the stage where it is profusely frothing or dripping on the ground. Although it can likely be caused by bit chewing it does often present without any active bit playing.

Salivate Heavy

Ref: Var.7   Impact Value   1.02

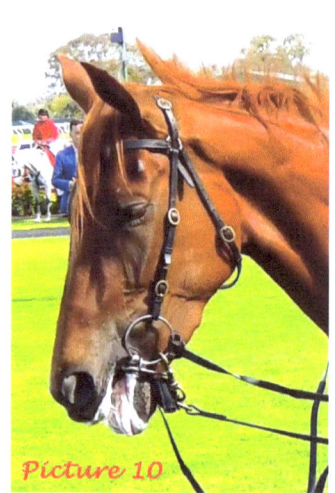

The overall impact value returned is near normal for the population but when broken down into sprinters up to 1200 metres or 6 furlongs the IV dropped to 0.55. A word of warning though because the observations in this subgroup of sprinters was under a hundred and this data size is probably not enough for reasonable accuracy.

The condition is identified by the horse heavily frothing and bubbling with saliva at the mouth (Picture 10) to the point where it is dripping to the ground. Bit chewing is usually present but not necessarily to a vigorous degree to cause the heavy salivation.

Still Mouth

Ref: Var.8   Impact Value   1.96

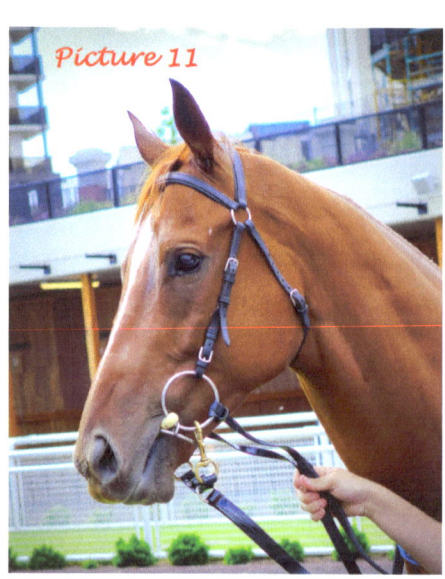

This is a strong positive factor evidenced by an Impact Value of 1.96 and is a very desirable trait across sprinter, miler and stayer alike. Refer to Picture 1 at the beginning of the chapter and Picture 11 for a good example of how the factor presents.

It is characterised by a closed mouth with comfortable, pliable lips and nostrils. The horse rarely chews on the bit and there is no sign of muscle tension or wrinkling anywhere. The horse will parade the whole time with a static mouth and is usually accompanied by a well-behaved walk and sensible demeanour.

The Still Mouth horse is telling us he is very comfortable and most importantly breathing correctly. This factor often translates into a horse that breathes and travels well in a race and hence conserves energy.

Head Toss

Ref: Var.9   Impact Value   0.78

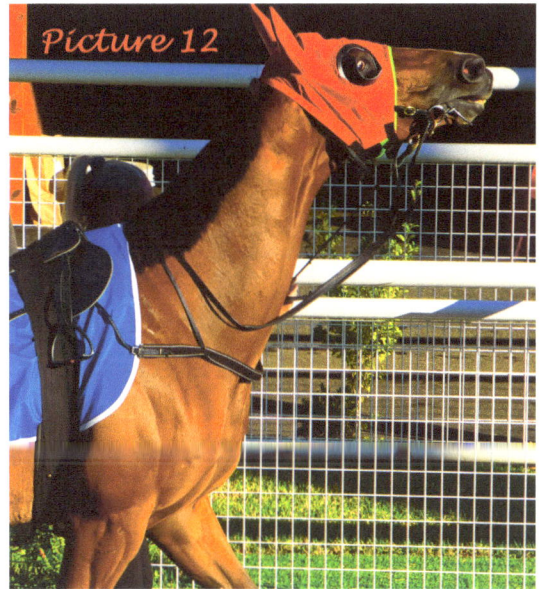

This is an easily identifiable factor. It can range from the horse throwing the head from its chest to way up high to elevating the head and doing short sharp shakes that causes the bit to bang against the teeth producing an audible sound. It can be quite violent at times and dangerous to groom and rider and very difficult to manage.

Probably more common in an up and down motion but some horses will throw the head east and west too. It's not a behaviour that instils confidence and may be a sign of nervousness, pain or apprehension in the horse. As one can imagine it has a negative Impact Value and is often associated with other undesirable behaviours.

"At The Yard Checklist" – Head Factors

Does the horse have any headgear changes or additions?

Does a factor intensify after the rider mounts?

What are the ear positions?

Is the mouth, muzzle, lips, nostrils, chewing muscles and brow all holding normal shape?

Is there a horse displaying Still Mouth?

Do the eyes look bright or is there white showing?

Is the horse head tossing?

Is the horse bit chewing excessively?

Can you hear bit grinding in any horse?

Is there any salivation? Is it mild or heavy?

Is the factor consistently displayed?

Is the horse telling me it is "head comfortable" or not?

Chapter 4. Factors of the Neck and Shoulder

The neck of the horse is vitally important in determining a horse's ability to move at its optimum capability. The position and angle of the neck influences where the centre of mass is, and the balance and fluency of the animal's stride.

It also contains the windpipe, and incorrect neck posture through the gaits can affect the efficiency of the respiratory system and hence proper breathing.

As pre-race horse watchers we are trying to assess the muscle development and carriage angles of the neck to ascertain information on how the horse has responded to its training and racing program. Positive responses to training regimens will show in the exposure of obvious muscle definitions and developments while adverse responses can be observed in weak muscle development and neck shapes. Negative results can be due to soreness, poor riding, the gear used or overtraining, but whatever the reason, the neck is one of the important components that help us identify the condition of the horse.

Neck Positive

Ref: Var.10   Impact Value   1.93

Picture 13 above is a good example of positive muscle definition of a horse's neck. There is a nice straight top line along the mane and then the first line of definition appears going over the groom's head and back into the withers. The next line appears through the middle of the neck into the groom's face and along this line are notches where the supporting ligaments of the neck attach. The underside shows a comfortably hanging windpipe with no restriction from any muscle tension from above it.
It's reasonable to assume from the muscle definition and comfortable carriage position that this horse has been positively responsive to its training program.

Picture 14 is another good example of a well-muscled neck due to positive acquisition from its training and racing program. More of a sprinter type neck compared to the longer leaner staying style in Picture 13.

Note the broad base of the neck as it runs neatly into the shoulder. One can sense the power and strength of the horse's development. The notches along the centre line are clearly visible here too.

This degree of positive muscle definition means the horse has been training very well with a good action free from anything affecting it and as the strong Impact Value denotes, it is a very desirable factor to see in the racehorse. They won't muscle up correctly like this if their galloping action is off due to soreness or other problems and when they achieve this level of definition they are at a very competitive level of fitness.

Neck Negative

Ref: Var.11   Impact Value   0.61

In Picture 15 the neck presents as very underdeveloped. There is no evident centreline muscle definition, which generally appears first and is very light in muscle bulk. These types of necks tend to portray a "gawky" appearance and are sometimes known as a "reverse" neck.

The angle of the neck is very elevated creating muscle tension on the underside of the neck. It's the opposite of the windpipe areas in Pictures 13 and 14 where neck carriage and muscle development allow for an unrestricted, relaxed and comfortable windpipe surround.

Light, weak looking necks tend to be accompanied by other underdeveloped areas of the horse such as shoulders and rear ends. Basically, they are part of the makeup of an animal that is struggling with the requirements of their training program and hence the low Impact Value.

Neck Arched

Ref: Var.12   Impact Value   1.38

An arched neck is a very positive attribute for a horse to display and is reflected in a handy Impact Value. It portrays a strong, proud and powerful profile much like a stallion strutting his stuff.

The topline of the neck curves towards the ears or poll area and the forehead is vertical or in this picture 16, behind the vertical and towards the chest.

It is often partnered with the horse walking up on its toes or "jig-jogging". If the jig-jogging walk is very much controlled and in no way unruly the horse shouldn't be negatively marked for its walk. The combination of these two factors in this manner is a display of readiness and strength from the horse.

Neck Twisted

Ref: Var.13   Impact Value   1.50

This is a common profile a lot of horses seem to take on. The neck topline is usually around horizontal and the nose is turned towards the groom and the ears point diagonally away from the groom. It probably could be defined as more of a head twist but when viewed from the front or rear you can see the twist in the neck.

The horses are generally very compliant on the lead when doing this and can often turn their heads right around into the groom's chest, especially if they are wearing blinkers. I've often sensed that the horses that do this seem very kind types and it's as if they are looking to their groom for guidance.

To take up this posture means that they must be feeling free in their muscles up front. To flex at the poll and twist the neck like they do and maintain it for a complete parade indicates they are comfortable doing it. Although the neck carriage may look awkward it's a positive action with a healthy 1.5 Impact Value.

Neck Horizontal

Ref: Var.14   Impact Value   1.14

Picture 18 depicts the typical profile of a horse that parades the yard maintaining a horizontal neck. From the ears along the mane to the withers, where the saddle cloth begins, that topline is parallel to the ground.

Carrying the neck in this position is a sign that the horse isn't feeling anything, that muscular wise, may inhibit its performance, such as soreness. Dropping the neck to this position pulls on muscles further through

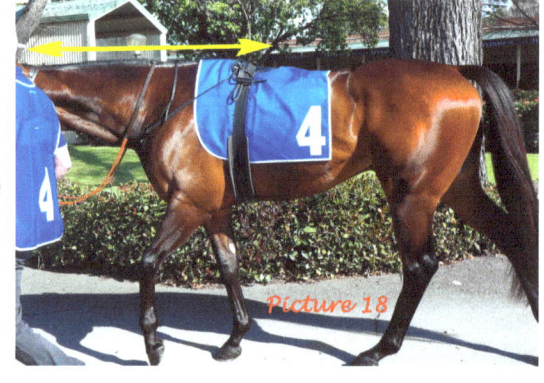

to the rear and like us humans with sore backs, the head would be lifting if pain was being felt. You will often hear these horses described as very relaxed and chilled out and they are. It's a great pointer that the horse will perform to its best, the investor can at least deduce that the horse is very comfortable within itself.

Ground Licker

Ref: Var.15   Impact Value   1.71

This neck carriage is a trait I really like to see. It has a very high Impact Value.

The horse drops its neck way down to a position where the mouth is close to touching the ground. They usually do it for 10 to 30 metres or so during the parade and occasionally they will keep trying to do it after the jockey has mounted.

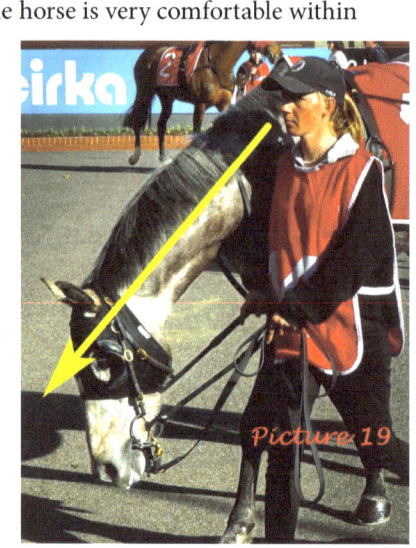

It's often accompanied with a strong purposeful walk. A lot of grooms try to keep pulling the head up to stop them doing it which in turn often ends in a bit of a tussle. In Picture 19 the groom has just let the horse drop the neck and avoided any confrontation with it.

This profile is a definite indication that the horse is feeling free and unencumbered by any soreness or niggles from the rigorous training they go through as it requires a good degree of suppleness to do it. Equine physios and massage therapists even encourage stretching exercises where the head is positioned back through the front legs to help flexibility. It's another positive indicator to include in the paddock watcher's arsenal.

The Average Neck

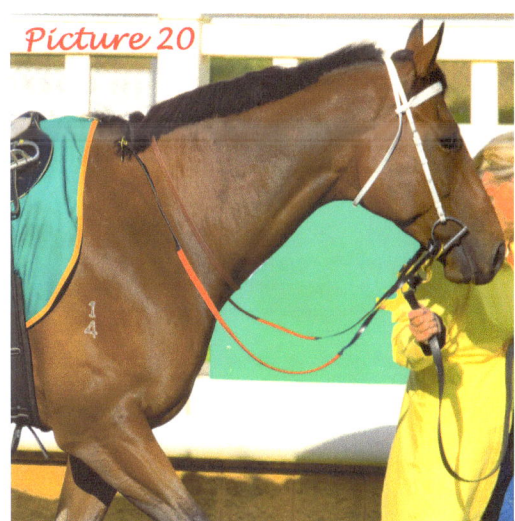

So far, we've looked at muscle definitions and carriage profiles of the neck from the positive and negative aspects. So, what would the basic, or default neck, look like?

Looking at the topline of the neck in Picture 20 the angle to the ground is about the most common carriage position you would see. There is a hint of muscle definition starting to appear in the middle of the neck along where a defined centre line would be but overall, it is blank and absent of any strong muscle definition as in Picture 13. On the other side of an assessment this is definitely not a negative neck. In fact, there is good development of muscle bulk and a wide base blending into the shoulder. The shoulder also is blank, matching the neck, but this horse is not far away from being marked as a positive neck.

When marking horses at the yard I've never had a category for the basic or default neck type, I have just marked the positives and negatives either side of it. However, by removing all the data for the neck types I have marked, and assuming the remainder were Average neck types, the Impact Value returned is 1.03. Very close to normal for the population as one may expect.

Prior to moving on to the shoulder description there is an important observation relating to the neck carriage that should be mentioned. The lower the neck carriage the higher the Impact Value. This extends from an extreme elevated neck, which often falls into the Head Toss category, down through the Average angle to the Horizontal and on to the Ground Licker. This graduation in Impact Value strength highlights the benefit of being able to identify these factors from the parade ring.

Shoulder Positive

Ref: Var.16   Impact Value   1.3

It's clear from pictures 21 and 22 that a positive shoulder is comprised of good definition and some muscle bulk. These are obviously quality animals with well-conditioned muscles and you're not going to see this at every yard you observe at, but there are degrees of it for one to make comparisons across the competitors. The muscle bulk can be gauged by how far it sits up relative to the girth strap. Stayers may tend to have less bulk as they are generally a much leaner type, but I have seen thin horses in average condition where the muscles from the girth through to the chest hardly protrude higher than the girth.

Horses with good shoulder development and definition will usually have similar development in the neck and rear ends. Achieving this means they have been well loaded in their training, most likely galloping with a good action and gaining optimum acquisition from their program.

Chapter 4. Factors of the Neck and Shoulder

Picture 20 is a good example of an average or default shoulder development. Still a relatively blank appearance that one would consider not quite there yet.

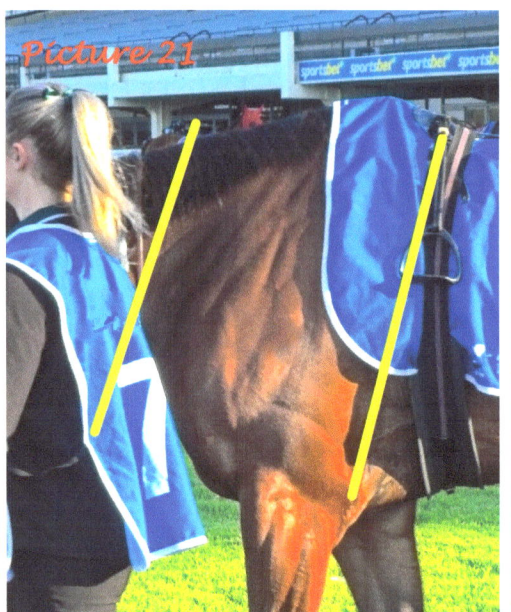

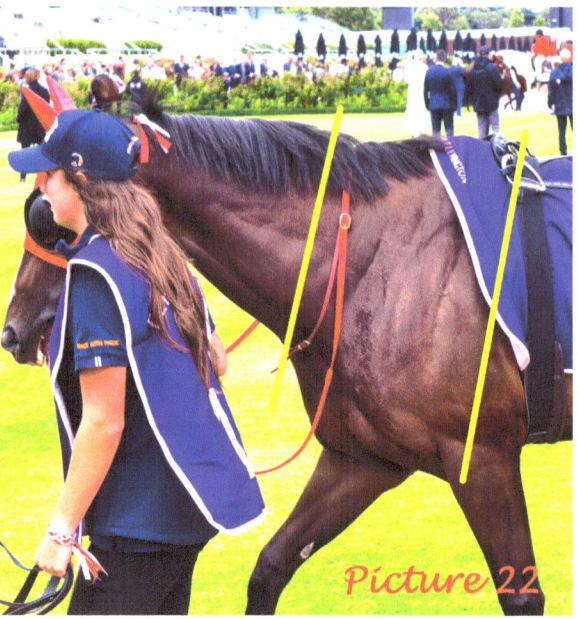

"At The Yard Checklist" – Neck and Shoulder Factors

What degree of muscle definition do the neck and shoulder display?

Are they highly defined, starting to show and coming along or blank?

Does the neck appear weak? No muscle bulk.

Does the shoulder appear flat? No muscle bulk.

Is the neck arched?

Is the neck twisted?

Is the horse parading with a horizontal neck topline?

Is the horse ground licking?

Does the horse assume the average neck carriage position? 45 degrees to the ground.

Chapter 5. Factors of the Mid-Section

The Mid-Section encompasses the area from the girth line behind the shoulder through to the flanks. The main structural component of this section is the rib cage, and we can use it to determine a level of fitness in the horse. Not so much by muscle definition as has been described in the neck and shoulder regions, but by visibility of the ribs.

The spine or backbone runs through this area too and is a very important structure to consider. The topline should be broad and flat and connect seamlessly into the rear end.
Horses in poor condition will lose the muscles around the spine causing it to begin to become exposed.

Unfortunately, I haven't marked this area, as over the years saddlecloths have tended to get bigger and bigger, leaving less and less of the topline visible. However, whatever the topline condition is, strong or weak, it is usually partnered with the equivalent condition in the rear end, so assessments are accounted for there.

Rib Cage Positive

Ref: Var.17   Impact Value   1.8

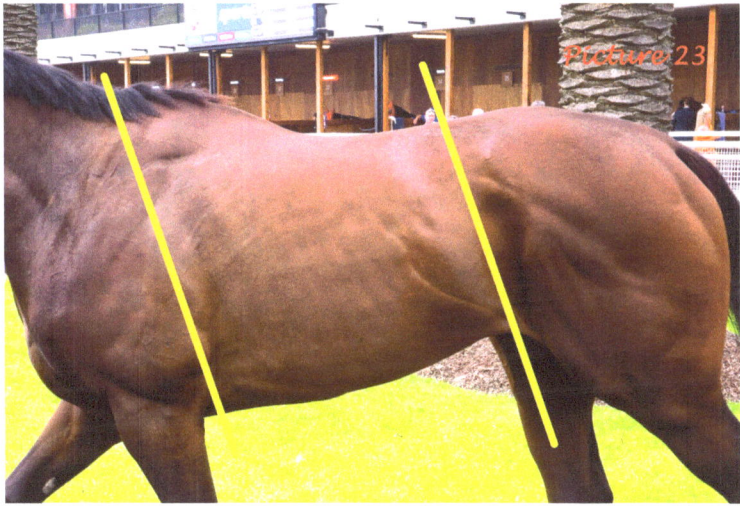

Picture 23 is of a quality staying type that was contesting a stakes race and is a good depiction of a positive rib cage for that style of horse.

The outline of the ribs is visible through a lean coverage of tissue while still maintaining a flat topline. This is the optimum level of rib visibility for distance horses, but sprinters and milers tend to have slightly more coverage of condition over the rib cage, but you still should be able to see the rib outline. This is a good area to assess the fitness of the horse as there are degrees of rib cage visibility ranging from what is shown in Picture 23 to not being able to see any rib outline at all indicating a horse short of peak fitness and race readiness.

This is an area where the horse watcher should really try to develop an eye for being able to assess the horse's fitness at a brief glance. Saddlecloths do inhibit getting a full view of the rib cage but with experience a reasonable valuation can still be made in the areas below and behind the saddlecloth. Those that have access to the stalls or saddling area may be able to view the horses prior to them being saddled.

The importance of being competent in assessing the rib cage as part of the overall fitness make up is reflected in the strong Impact Value.

Chapter 5. Factors of the Mid-Section

Rib Cage Negative

Ref: Var.18   Impact Value   0.73

Here we are dealing with the other side of the rib cage spectrum and once again the low Impact Value exemplifies the importance of a good evaluation of it.

The negative rib cage is marked when there is no visual evidence of the ribs. In Picture 24, behind the saddlecloth and below, clearly shows no sign of rib outline as it is covered with a layer of fat. The blank appearance of what we can see of the rib cage area equates with the lack of muscle definition of the shoulder and the rear end. It's reasonable to say that this horse is not yet near its optimum race fitness.

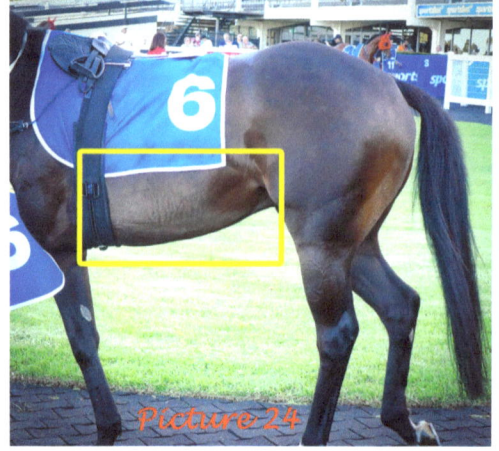

Tension Line

Ref: Var.19   Impact Value   0.74

A Tension Line appears as a distinct muscle crease that runs from the girth back to the rear of the stomach just above the underbelly profile and occurs through tightening of the abdominal muscles. There is an airway condition called Heaves that presents similarly but it won't be the reason you see it on horses at the track. It appears when a horse is passing a motion, and horses often show it intermittently during a parade which is normal. I only mark it if it is consistently displayed as I've always thought it is a sign that the horse is bracing itself against something it may be feeling. I've also noticed it on a few horses where it occurs on only one side and without any sign of lameness.

Underbelly Negative

Ref: Var.20   Impact Value   0.45

As Picture 26 depicts this factor is easy to identify. The belly hangs down in an obvious arc instead of gradually rising in a straighter line as it heads rearwards.

It is seen a lot in gross type horses that are returning from a spell and require racing to bring them to competitive fitness. It's probably equivalent to the human pot belly. There are some horses that naturally do carry a heavy underbelly, even distance types, and it's probably a matter of knowing they're like that from having previously seen them and so not marking them for the category.

The condition is clearly due to a lack of fitness and it's no surprise to see the very low Impact Value.

Chapter 5. Factors of the Mid-Section

Flanks Negative

Ref: Var.21   Impact Value   0.68

The adjacent picture is a good example of negative flanks. The highlighted region shows the hollowed-out appearance of the flanks that constitutes the marking of this factor. It is normally associated with other poor attributes like muscle bulk starting to fall away from the spine, hip protrusion, weak thighs and a generally weak back end. It's one of the signs that the horse may have come to the end of its preparation.

As you would expect it carries a very low Impact Value and along with the previous factor, Underbelly Negative, they almost warrant immediate removal from being any real competitive chance or selection choice.

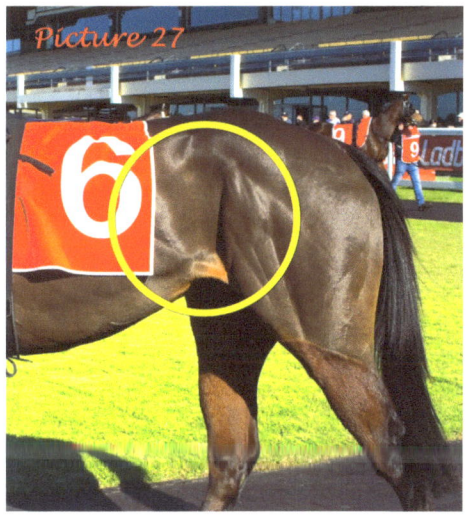

"At The Yard Checklist" – Mid Section Factors

Are the ribs partially visible with a slight coverage of condition?

Was the race for sprinters and was an allowance made for slightly more condition over the rib cage?

Are the ribs covered with layers of fat and not visible at all?

Has any horse paraded consistently displaying a tension line?

Has any horse presented with a clearly hanging underbelly?

Did any of the horses appear to have flanks that were hollowed out or sucked in?

Chapter 6. Factors of the Rear End

This section is "the big end of town" so to speak. It is one of the most influential factors on performance. The neck and shoulder have a high contribution to balance and reach in the stride whereas the rear end supplies the power and drive. Both ends working in harmony lead to optimum stride and performance. Similarly, there's usually harmony between the front and rear muscle development too. Generally, if the rear end has positive development the front end will also and the same applies to poor development.

Important muscle development takes place in the area during the horse's training and racing program, and it is vital that the horse watcher can identify and grade the positive and negative changes that occur here. Also, for regular watchers who know or keep records of their observations they have the advantage of being able to detect change from previous assessments. Has the horse improved, regressed or held its condition from past parade ring observations?

As was done in the neck and shoulder descriptions of the front end, muscle definition and bulk are the method used to assess the various factors of the rear end. Muscles of the racehorse in training can generally be put into three categories, anabolic, where the horse is gaining muscle, holding muscle condition, and catabolic, where the horse is in a phase of depletion of muscle. These are all responses to racing and training that we try to identify from our pre-race judgements. We don't need to know the cause of them we just need to be able to pick them.

The descriptions and pictures used here are for the positive and negative extremes of muscle development of the rear end. The majority of the horses parading will fall within those boundaries. Using the extremes makes it easier to understand where each side of the default or basic development is heading and therefore enable grading of assessments accordingly.

We'll begin with some positive and negative muscle definitions then go through details of the negatively built rear ends and on to the positive rear end builds.

Money Mark Positive

Ref: Var.22   Impact Value   1.52

The Money Mark is an easily distinguishable crease that starts at the point of the hip and slopes diagonally downwards towards the rear. It is a good gauge of rear end muscle development progression as it will be barely visible in a fat unfit horse, shallow and just visible in the semi fit horse and then well defined in the fit horse as seen in Picture 28. It is also visible in the thin horse but presents as a very tight, pencil thin line because of the lack of muscle surrounding it.

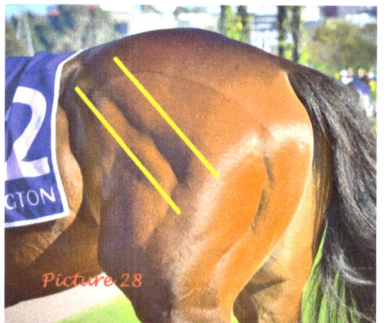

Money Mark Negative

Ref: Var.23   Impact Value   0.74

The rear end in Picture 29 is in direct contrast to the positive Money Mark example in Picture 28. There is not even a hint of a crease developing and the whole area is blank. The horse is clearly at a lesser stage of fitness from racing and training than that of the horse in Picture 28. The criteria for marking a negative Money Mark were as the picture depicts, it isn't visible. It is an obvious sign of a horse short of fitness and is reflected in the low Impact Value.

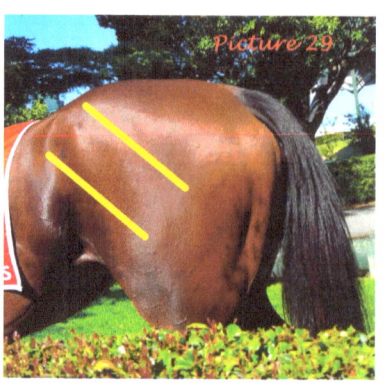

Chapter 6. Factors of the Rear End

Racing Dimple Positive

Ref: Var.24   Impact Value   1.64

The Racing Dimple originates at the tail head and runs down towards the leg, branching into two creases halfway down the rear end. In a well-conditioned horse, it should be clearly defined along its entire length.

Like the Money Mark it is also apparent in thin horses and presents as a very thin tight line due to the lack of surrounding muscle bulk. Picture 30 is a good example as you can see the curvature of some muscle bulk as it comes away from the dimple crease.

Along with the Money Mark it is a good reference point for assessing rear end development.

Racing Dimple Negative

Ref: Var.25   Impact Value   0.74

Compare this to the positive Racing Dimple picture and it's easy to see the difference. Here the only sign of any development of the dimple is the hint of a crease in the lower branch area and that depression is usually visible in all horses.

As the horse increases in fitness condition, and the dimple becomes defined, the upper singular part tends to develop and show more and more towards the tail head. In the leaner staying types, the upper end tends to go right to the tail head and in sprinters and more heavily muscled types it may not reach that far.

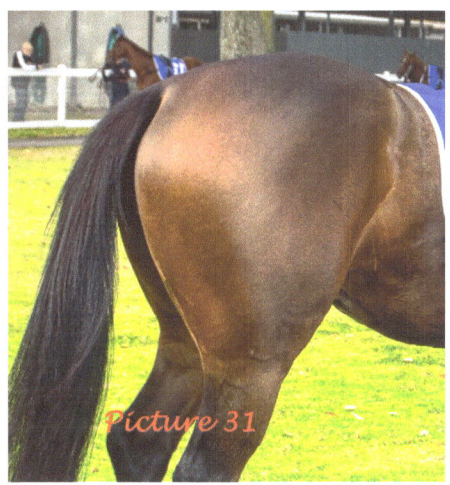

What has been shown here, and marked accordingly, across both the positive and negative Racing Dimple factors are the extremes of its appearance or non-appearance. As with all muscle definitions there are graduations between the boundaries that apply as fitness of the horse progresses or regresses and with experience the yard watcher can become very accurate with fitness analysis.

Rump Top Negative

Ref: Var.26   Impact Value   0.56

Pictures 32/33 are examples of muscle depletion or poor development of the rear end that are typical of horses that should be categorised as Rump Top Negative. From the point of the hip, signified by the yellow circle, to the peak of the spine at the yellow arrowhead, there is no build-up of muscle. It is flat from hip to spine. If you can visualise looking at the profile from directly behind the horse it would look like an inverted "V" shape.

The red arrows depict how the muscles fall away flatly from the topline. The whole rear end structure is absent of any well-developed muscle bulk.

Chapter 6. Factors of the Rear End

The Impact Value is a very low 0.56, reflective of the lack of power and drive that this profile produces. There are always exceptions to the rule, but the ability and knowledge to be able to recognise the factor, and with practice, degrees of it, is an asset on the watcher's side.

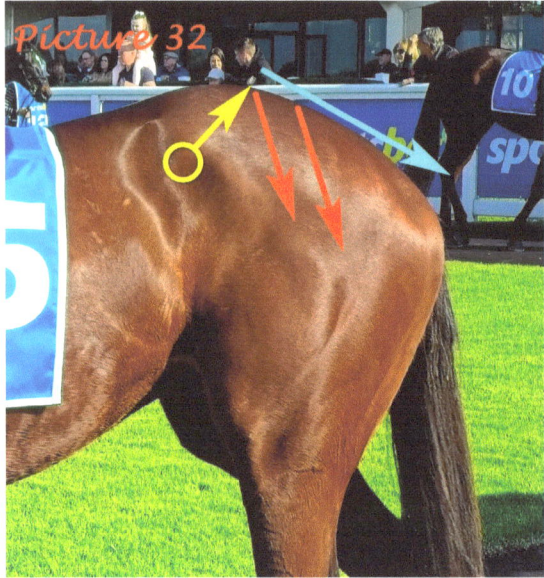
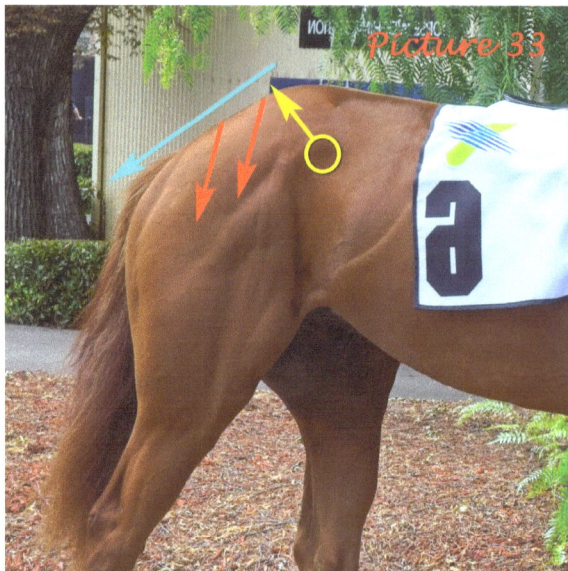

Hip Pointing

Ref: Var.27   Impact Value   0.68

Hip pointing is when protrusion of the point of the hip starts to occur through depletion of the muscles.

The point of the hip is located at the top of the Money Mark where the red arrowhead is inside the yellow circle of Picture 34.

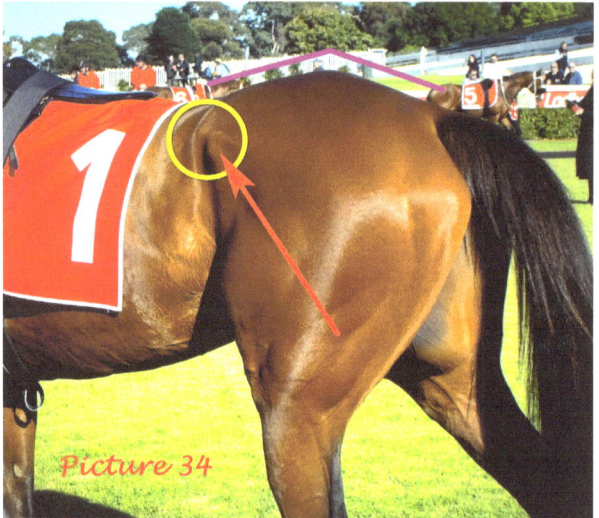

After viewing thousands of horse rear ends my belief is that – "Hip Point = Turning Point". What that means is that protrusion of the hip is the first sign that a horse may have "had enough", as is commonly mentioned, and is starting to regress in condition. Its presence coincides with the beginning of the rear end becoming more angular and less round. There is a decline of muscle "build" above the hip point causing the prominence of the hip to occur. This angularity is depicted in Picture 34 by the pink lines. As we work through descriptions of the positive rear end signs, the contrast between a hip pointer and a horse with "build" will become clearer.

Hip pointing is a very important feature to identify and has an Impact Value of 0.71. When marking this feature, I can say that I was a very harsh judge too. As soon as I detected a hint of protrusion, even from very robust sprinting horses, short priced horses and runners in group races, its presence was marked, and the low IV figure probably vindicates the harsh marking and importance of its identification.

Chapter 6. Factors of the Rear End

Thigh Negative

Ref: Var.28   Impact Value   0.6

A low Impact Value for the negative thigh is not unexpected, as it is in tune with the results for the other rear end negative factors.

As you follow the arrows down in Picture 35 from the halfway area of the rear end towards the hock, the muscle load is very light. And if viewed from behind the horse, under the tail, a large gap would be obvious between the lean inner thighs, whereas on a strong back ended horse the inner thighs would almost be rubbing together.

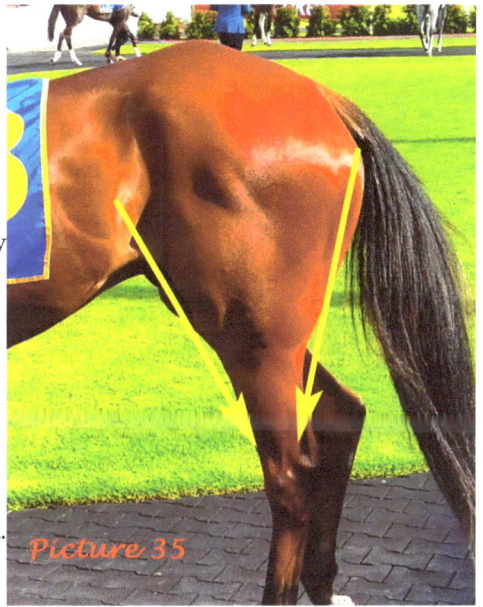

If you're seeing the other weak structures of the rear, as we are in the picture, like hollow flanks, hip pointing and poor rump top, you're most definitely going to see a thin thigh area. All the negative factors behind the saddle usually go hand in hand together and one can sense the lack of drive and power they convey.

Rump Top Positive

Ref: Var.29   Impact Value   2.31

Positive Rump Top is the factor where the power of the rear end resides. Just like everything below a negative rump top usually follows suit with poor muscle strength, the structures below a positive rump top will exhibit strength and bulk, as Picture 36 demonstrates.

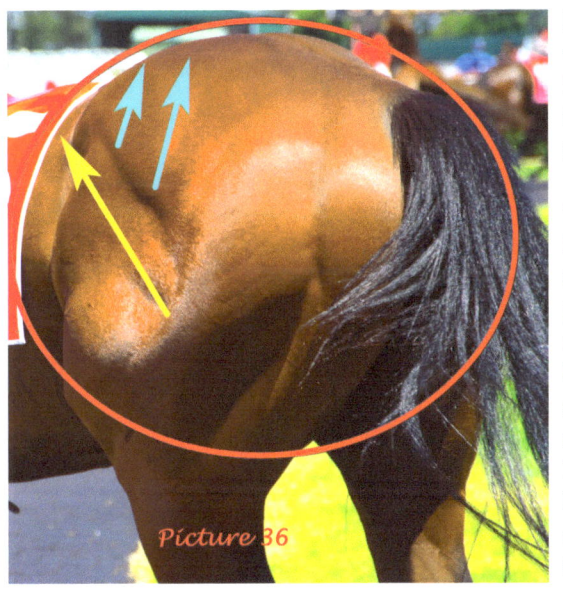

Prior to describing how to identify the factor it's worth noting the stark difference between Picture 32/33 and 36. A good example of the extremes, from the thin angular to the well-muscled and rounded rear end.

The area of the factor is defined within the red circle. If you follow the yellow arrow along the Money Mark to its head at the point of the hip, there is no hip point protrusion, and the blue arrow depicts where the muscle "build" occurs. From the top of the Money Mark upwards should be nearly a vertical wall of muscle. This is the key to marking the factor and is more obvious in the rear 45-degree angle of Picture 37, shown by the blue arrows. This picture also shows how the muscle bulk rounds around to the slight depression of the spine. There should be no direct line from the point of the hip to the spine. It should firstly go vertically up where "build" has occurred and then arc over to the spine. The viewing angle of Picture 37 is my preferred look at the horse when assessing the factor at the parade ring. As the horse comes side on, I look for the Money Mark then as it moves away, I can check for any hip pointing and then assess the muscle build above that point and then the profile of the muscles rounding over to the spine.

Chapter 6. Factors of the Rear End

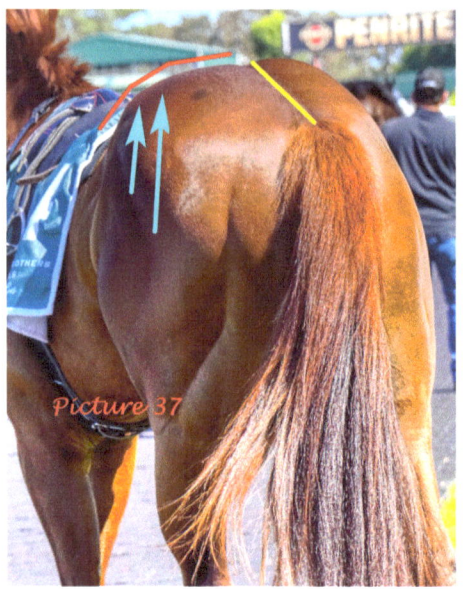

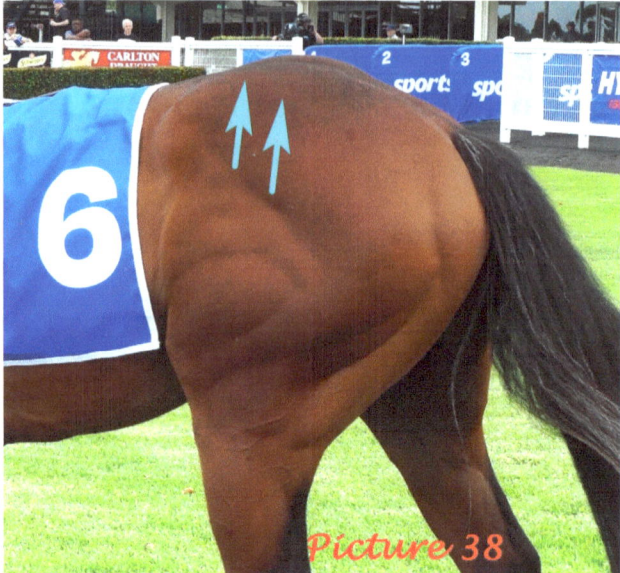

Picture 38 is of a naturally robust style of horse that was competing over sprint distances and was displaying a positive rump top due to a good degree of build above the point of the hip.

There is no denying how critical it is for a parade watcher to be able to identify a positive rump top with an exceptional Impact Value of 2.31. It takes a bit of practice but once mastered it can be assessed at a glance. The key features are no hip point exposure, a vertical build of muscle above the hip and a rounding of muscle over to the spine.

The Average Rear End

In this section I've described and pictured the good and bad extremes of the rear end. Most of the horses viewed at the mounting yard will land somewhere in between. Not worthy of being marked positive or negative. Hopefully the depictions explained here will enable the analyst to determine what side the horse's appearance is heading to.

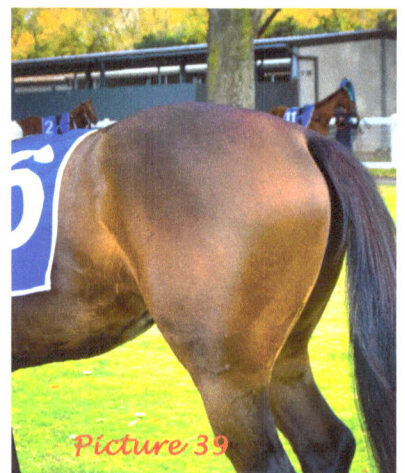

In Picture 39 the horse is heading towards the positive with a bit of branching down the bottom of the racing dimple but overall blank muscle definition. There's no obvious pronounced hip point and the general shape and profile is good. Just slightly short of optimum fitness I'd suggest and couldn't be marked for any of the rear end positive factors at that stage.

Tail Swishing

Ref: Var.30   Impact Value   0.98

The Impact Value implies that tail swishing is neither a positive nor negative trait but there are some considerations to be had. One consideration is to decipher if the cause is due to flies and insects or does it stem from a physical or mental irritation. With the fly scenario the whole field of horses are usually flicking their tails at the pests intermittently.

If it's due to a physical or mental issue it normally presents in tandem with another visible factor such

Chapter 6. Factors of the Rear End

as head tossing, unruly behaviour etc. This is dealt with further in the chapter on factor combinations. It may well be that you can't spot a paired factor with the swishing and flicking, and in this case, I would add more importance to its presence. When marking the trait, I did it on an all-in basis, if it swished it was marked. This may have caused some watering down of the Impact Value.

Normal carriage of the tail is when it sits slightly off the body at the tailhead, and the hair hangs freely and naturally as the horse walks.

Tail Jammed

Ref: Var.31   Impact Value   0.82

Here is a side on view of a tail wedged tightly into the backside crevice. Viewing from the rear can often show flaring of the tail hair as the stump is jammed hard into the rear. Referencing back to Picture 39 is a good example of the difference between a tucked tail and a comfortable free hanging one.

It is not the most common variable that one will come across, but it does have a mildly negative Impact Value and should be taken note of.

It's considered a sign of apprehension, submission, timidity and even frightened behaviour in a horse. Not the positive signs you'd associate with a ready and willing competitive animal.

Once again, I should mention that like all pre-race factors, they should be exhibited consistently, for the length of the animal's parade.

"At The Yard Checklist" – Rear End Factors

How did the Money Mark appear? Visible, coming along, blank?

How was the Racing Dimple graded?

How was the Rump Top assessed? Angular, average, muscled?

Was there muscle build above the point of the hip?

Was the hip protruding?

Was the thigh area light in muscle? Well-muscled?

What was the overall grading of the rear end development? Peak, coming along, light in muscle?

How was the tail carriage? Slightly off the rump and hanging comfortably, swishing, jammed?

Chapter 7. Putting It All Together-Whole Body Fitness Grading

Now that we have dissected the horse into sections, from head to tail, and looked at the components that can be utilised for judgements within those sections, the next step is to combine all the observations and categorise them into overall fitness gradings.

The categories used for this purpose are – Fit, Average, Fat, Thin.

Fitness assessments are the most common decisions that the yard analyst will make and should make. No need to explain the advantage of being able to identify a fit horse over an unfit horse. With practice and concentrated observation, it's possible to really refine the watcher's skills to a degree where one can separate fitness values within each category.

As an example, if you were using a rating or points system out of 100 and the Fit category occupied the upper quartile from 75 – 100 and you selected three horses from the parade as Fit, then with experience you can further grade those fitness assessments between the 75 and 100. Eventually, through a sharp eye and repetitive observations these distinctions of graduations will become second nature and can be done at a basic glance.

In making judgements on the fitness factors, only the muscle definition variables discussed in the previous chapters were used. Factors are based solely on muscle build or the lack of it. Behaviour, walking styles, sweating and other variables that will be looked at further ahead, were not a component of the fitness categories assessments.

Fit

Ref: Var.32   Impact Value   2.09

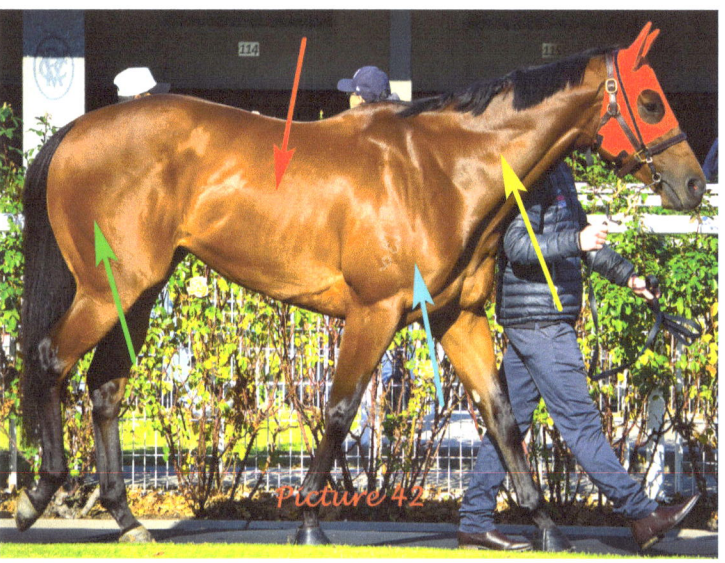

Picture 42 depicts a very fit, well-conditioned athletic horse, displaying all the attributes that constitute the yard analyst to grade it as "Fit". The muscle bulk and definitions immediately stand out as one views it. The neck (yellow arrow) has the criteria of a "positive neck" as described earlier, visible centre line with notches and a wide neck base neatly blending into the shoulder. Definition and muscle bulk acquisition is evident in the shoulder (blue arrow) and through the mid-section (red arrow) there is no hang in the underbelly nor any excessive cover of the rib cage. This mid-section flows well into the rear end (green arrow) which displays good development of the Money Mark and Racing Dimple. The Rump Top is nicely rounded and there is no evidence of angulation, Hip Pointing or hollow Flanks.

This obviously healthy horse has well balanced development from one end to the other and from this it would be safe to assume that the horse has been thriving in its work and definitely slots into the Fit category.

The horse in Picture 43 is another good example of a Fit racehorse. All the positives noted in Picture 42 are on display here too. Particularly in the rear end where the Positive Rump Top exudes power.

I hope these two pictures can serve to allay any doubts a beginner watcher may have on their ability to identify a fit ready racehorse, as once one is cognisant with the factors to look for, a glance at a single walk by in the parade ring is all that is

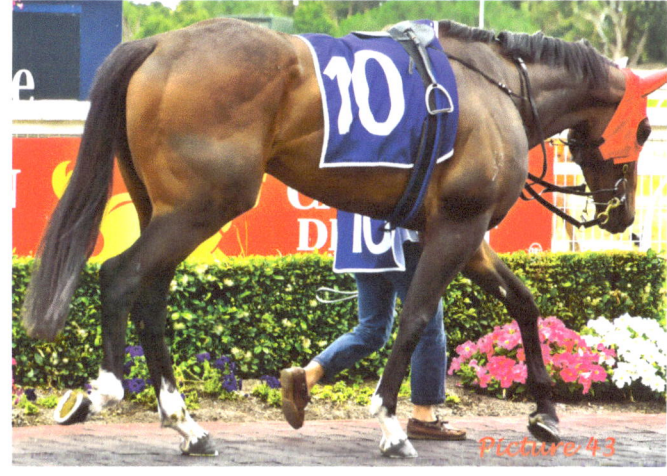

often needed, and I feel these pictures depict that. They stand out as being in the Fit category.

Average

Ref: Var.33   Impact Value   0.91

The Average fitness category is the one that many horses will slot into. They are at a stage of their preparations where they haven't peaked into the Fit bracket and are conditioned enough to avoid the Fat or Thin categories.

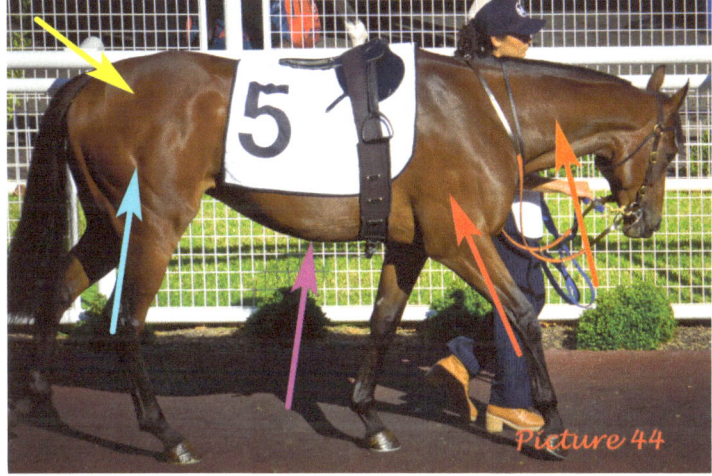

The pictures selected here represent nice horses at each end of the category range. Picture 44 is at the Fit end and the flashy sort in Picture 45 is at the Fat perimeter of the Average spectrum.

The horse in Picture 44 is in good condition although my assessment is that it's just a gallop short of going into the Fit range. Looking at the neck, shoulder, Racing Dimple and Money Mark structures, the early formation of the muscle definitions can be seen giving a strong hint of developing well but they aren't as distinct as the horse in the Fit pictures. The Ribcage and Underbelly may still have a slight layer of extra coverage on them, and the Rump Top has a good shape happening but may be a little soft.

Admittedly it is a very close call as to which bracket the assessment falls into, but it is a good example of how, with practice and a trained ability to observe and judge the parameters, a yard analyst can refine their assessments to tight graduations.

As mentioned, the horse in Picture 45 ranks towards the Fat end of the Average range. Looking at the areas of the neck, shoulder and Money Mark, virtually no creasing or definition has started to come through. The Racing Dimple has begun to appear, and it usually is the first marker that one sees. There's still some condition to come off the mid-section and the Rump Top area appears soft still. Flanks are filled in and there is no hip protrusion apparent. My assessment is that the horse is a race and some

Chapter 7. Putting It All Together-Whole Body Fitness Grading

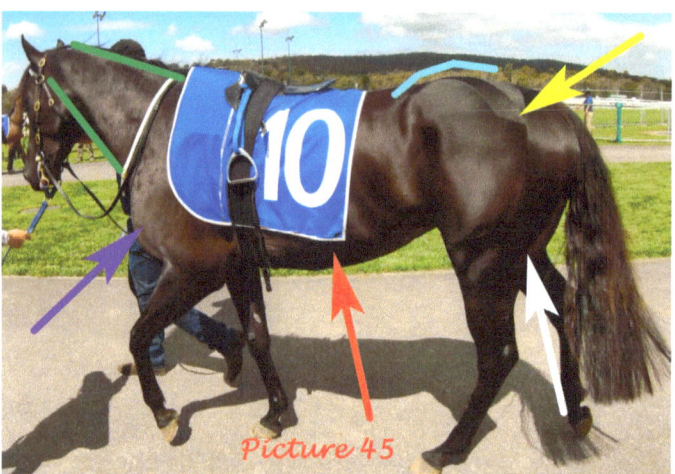

work away from optimum in its preparation but even though it is devoid of any developed muscle definitions, its overall shape suggests that it's on the right path forward. The blue arc depicts a strong shape developing into a possible positive Rump Top with some "build" from the point of the hip upwards. If there was greater hang to the Underbelly, that would definitely push it back into the Fat category.

Fat

Ref: Var.34   Impact Value   0.34

What we're dealing with here is "racehorse fat" and not like a recreational "paddock potato" pony may look when overweight. Even so, it's not hard to spot and is mainly characterised by heavy ribcage coverage, large Underbelly hang and the front and rear sections presenting very blank.

Commonly seen in horses returning from a break that are being raced into fitness, and even occurring in quality races with quality horses. Never let a quality horse with a good performance record deter you from judging it fat if that's how you grade it. Pre-race analysis at the parade ring is about the horse's condition in front of you, not what the form guide says.

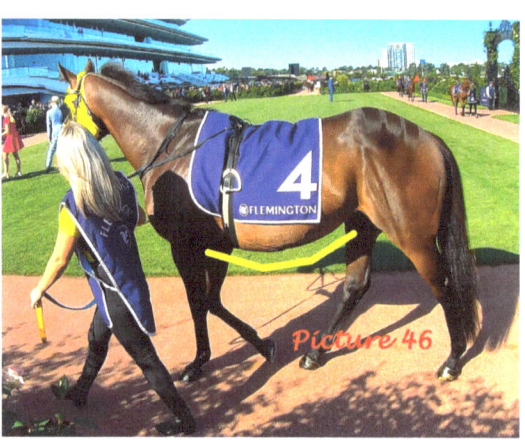 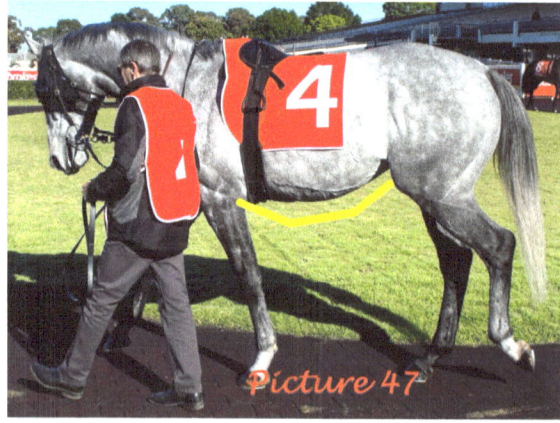

Thin

Ref: Var.35   Impact Value   0.45

In most instances the Thin grading will be determined by the rear end appearance. The horse in Picture 48 is no exception and should be clearly categorised as Thin.

There is no rounding of the Rump Top, it's very angular, and there is fall away from the spine. (Blue arc and arrows). The red arrow points to severe protrusion of the hip and the flanks present as hollow and sucked

Chapter 7. Putting It All Together-Whole Body Fitness Grading

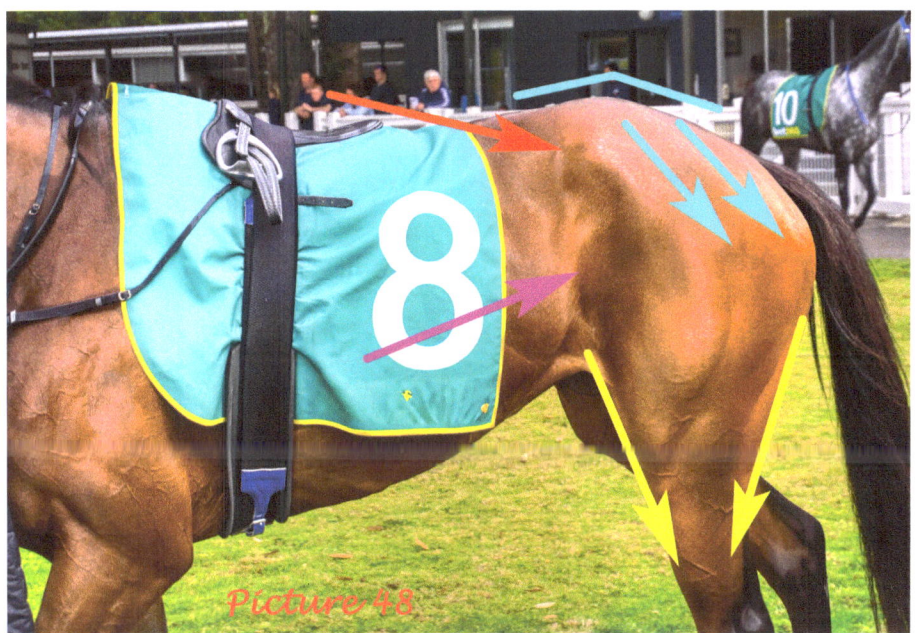

in. (pink arrow). As normally occurs with this upper hindquarter structure it leads down to very lean thigh muscles. (Yellow arrows).

The metrics emphasise the poor performance that horses in this category produce, with an Impact Value of 0.45 and a Win% of 4.4 they're definitely a risky investment.

Chapter 7. Putting It All Together-Whole Body Fitness Grading

Heads Positive

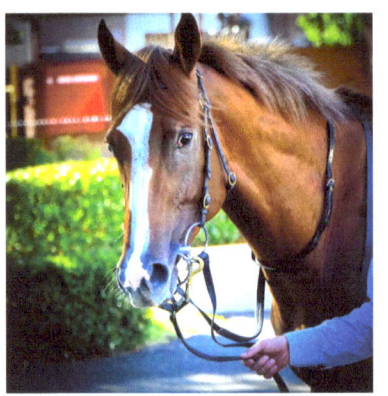

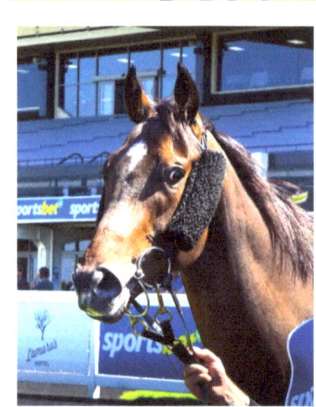

Heads Negative

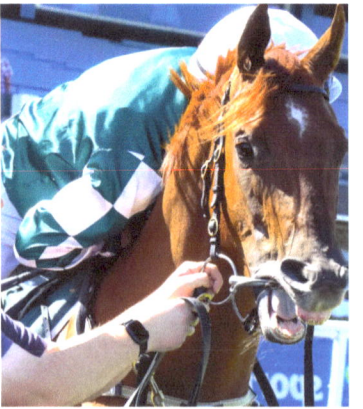
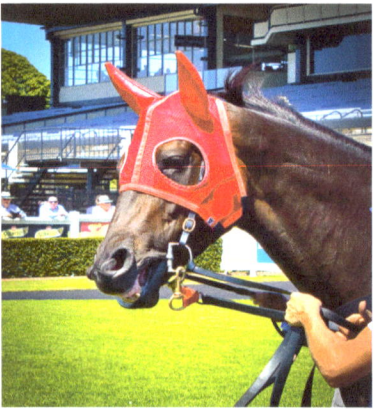

Chapter 7. Putting It All Together-Whole Body Fitness Grading

Shoulder and Neck Positives

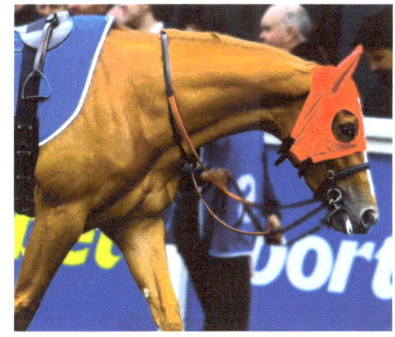

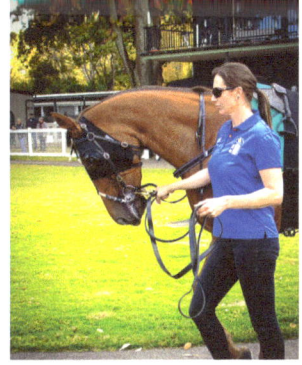
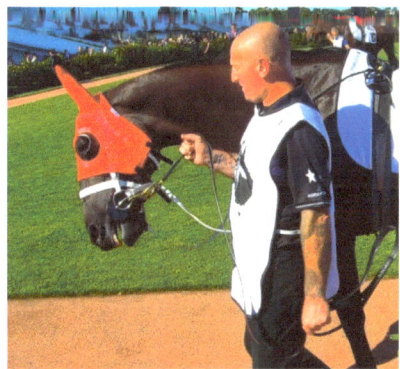

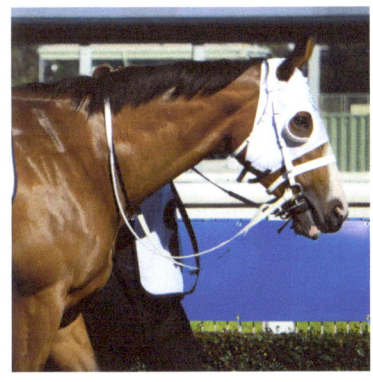
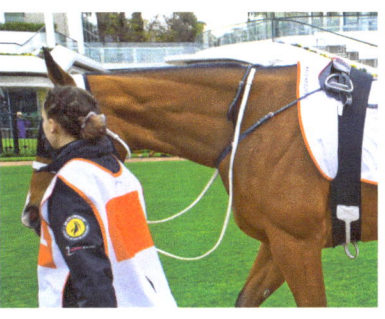
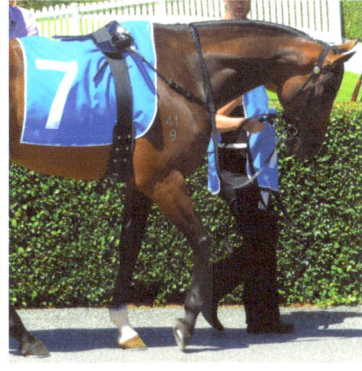

Chapter 7. Putting It All Together-Whole Body Fitness Grading

Underbelly Negative

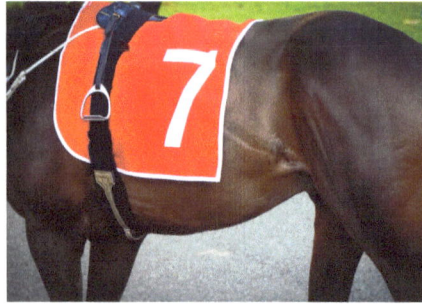
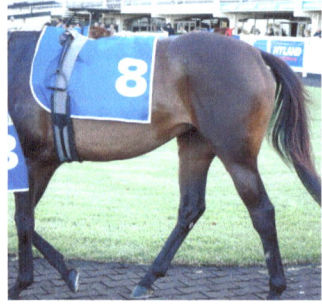

Flanks Negative

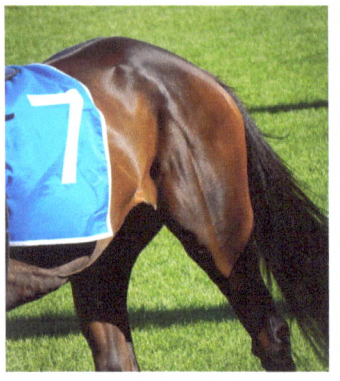
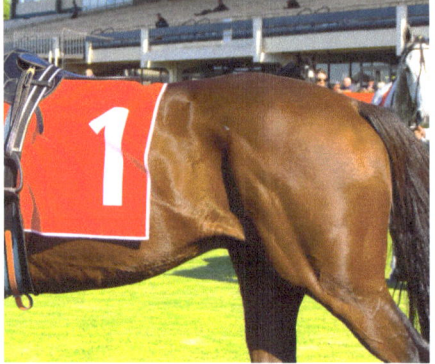
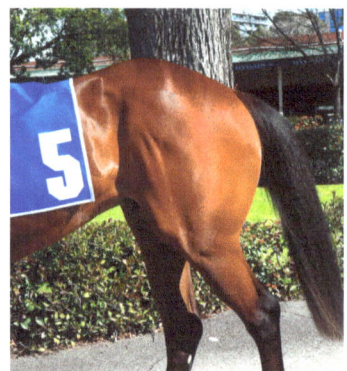

Hip Pointing and Angular Rear Ends

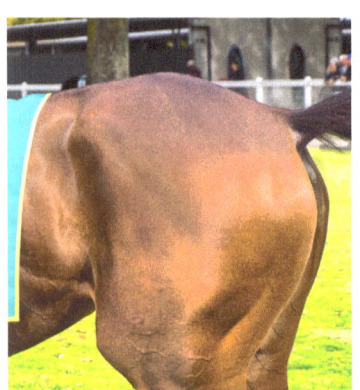

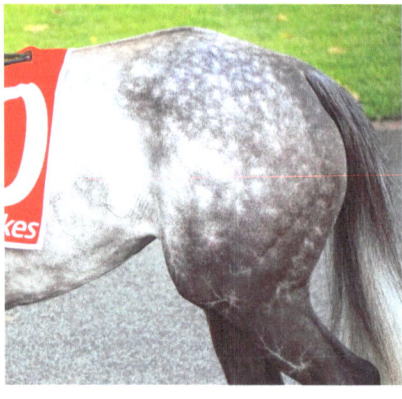
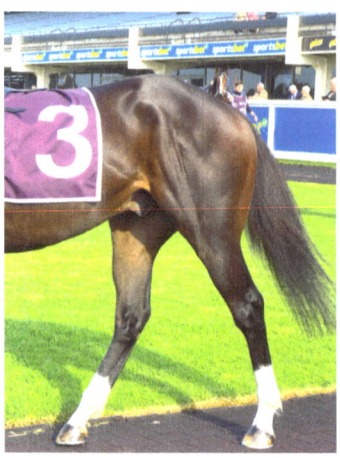

Chapter 7. Putting It All Together-Whole Body Fitness Grading

Rear Ends Coming Along

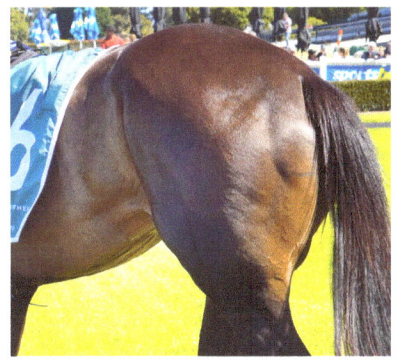
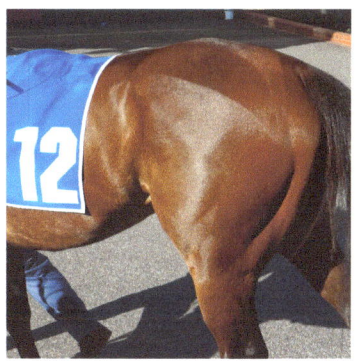
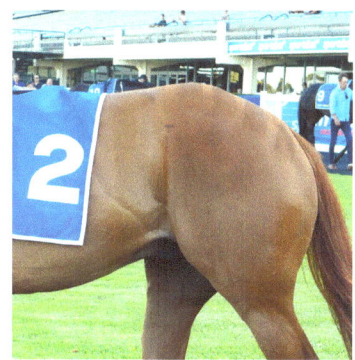

Feel The Power

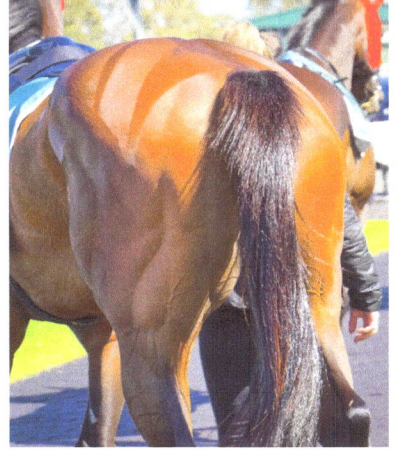
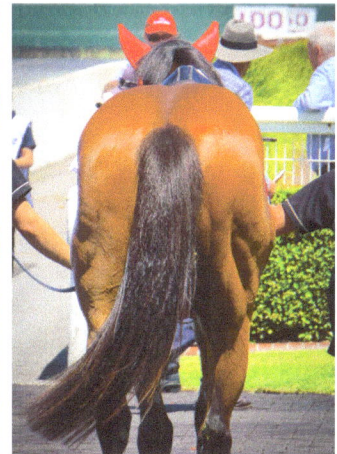
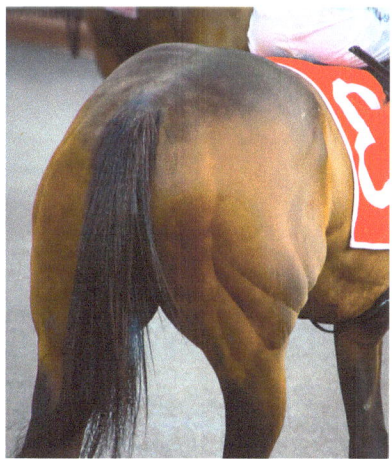

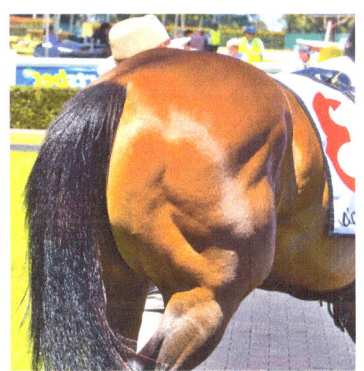
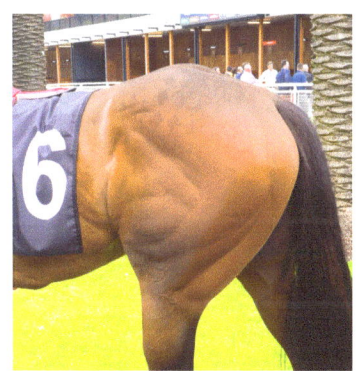
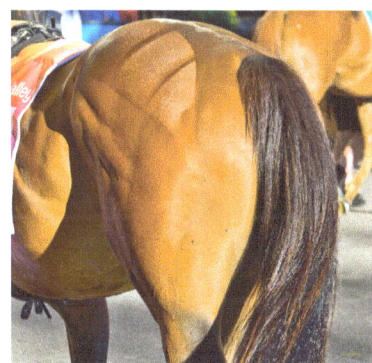

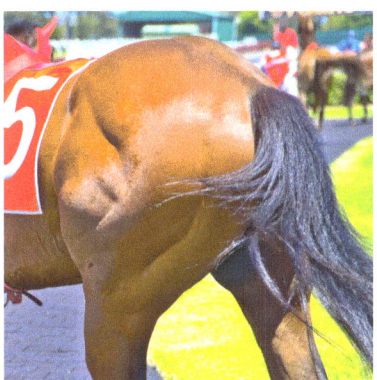
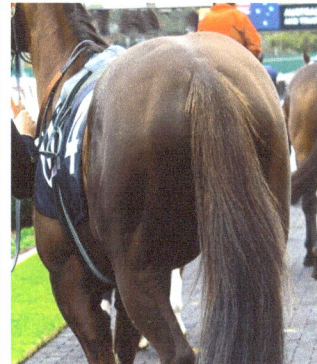
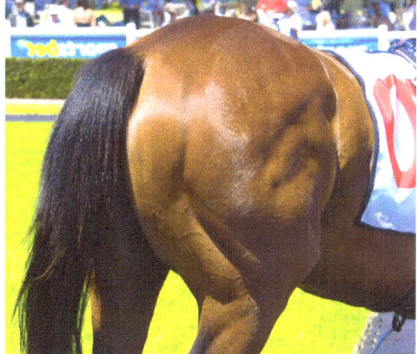

Chapter 7. Putting It All Together-Whole Body Fitness Grading

Close

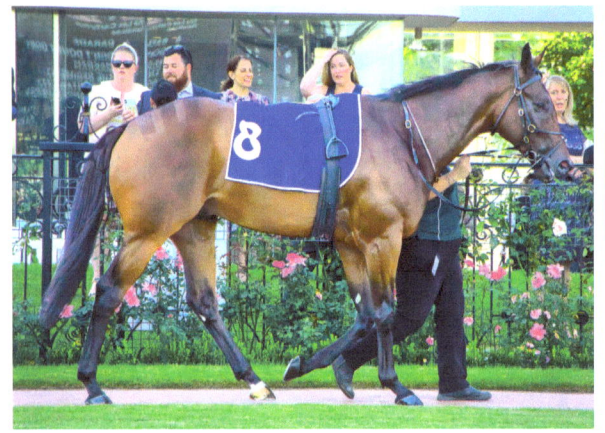
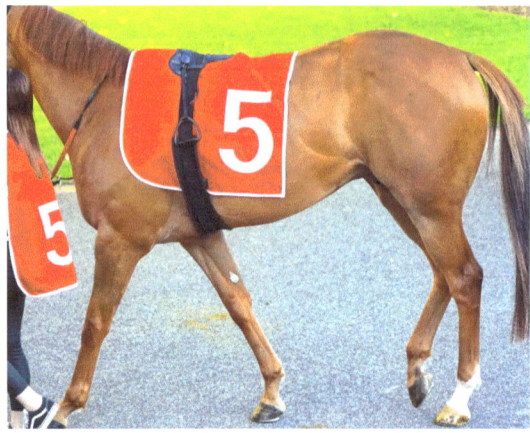

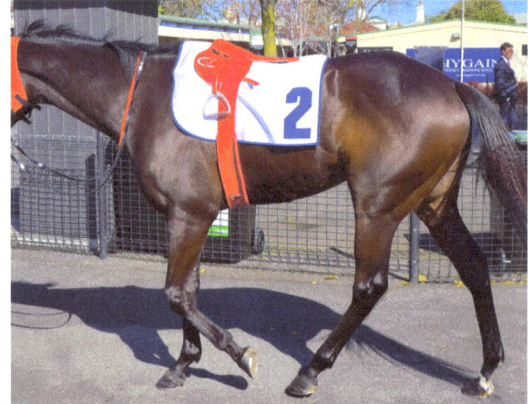

Well Developed

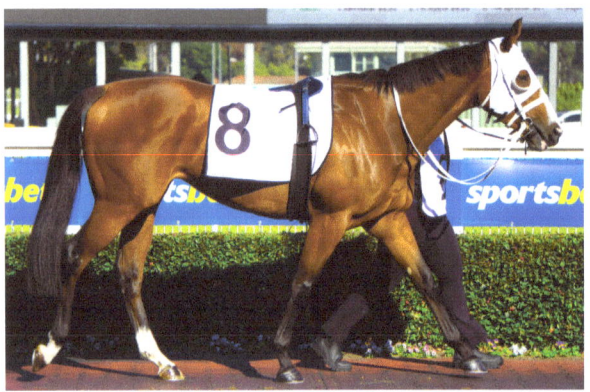

Chapter 8. Walking Styles

Racehorses present in the parade ring with a vast array of differing walking styles and the types that don't come under the classification of basic, average or normal will be described in this chapter and like most factors they range from the positive through to the negative. Some are naturally occurring for the horse and others may be due to physical and behavioural circumstances.

A horse's state of mind can often be judged by its walk.

Evaluating the peculiarities of various walks is essential for the horse watcher to master. It's important because walking styles correlate closely with how the racehorse is feeling both mentally and physically. Those free from any niggling injuries, muscle soreness etc may display a certain style of walk while those who may be feeling something physically may show a different walk. There's also those suffering from the race day experience mentally, due to apprehension, stress, heat, freshness or other factors that may cause changes to a normal walking style.

The thoroughbred has what's known as four "natural gaits". Walk, trot, canter and gallop. The trot is a "two beat" gait, meaning the landing pattern of the hooves is with the front and rear diagonals landing simultaneously. The canter is a "three beat" gait with a pair hitting the ground together and the other two independently. Both the walk and the gallop are "four beat" gaits. Each hoof landing independently and because of this relationship, an assessment of the pre-race walk may provide an insight into how the horse might gallop and stride during a race.

As the metrics tell us there is a strong relationship between positive walks and the angle of the neck carriage as described in an earlier chapter. Low neck carriage is a characteristic of a "Power Walk", as will be described further on, and a general rule is, the lower the neck angle in a walk, the more positive the walk is.

Some consideration must also be given to the type of horse being viewed and their walk. There is a tendency for stayers, or longer trip horses, to have lower neck carriages and bigger leg extensions at the walk, whereas the short course sprinting types are likely to have more upright neck carriage, and a shorter leg reach at the walk. It's probably due to their physical makeups, with the longer, leaner body type of the distance horse and the robust, short coupled style of the sprinting type. However, it is always a strong positive to see a sprinter, in a field of sprinters, drop his neck and flow around the parade ring.

So, the racehorse's walk can tell us about its physical well-being, its mental state and potentially about its galloping action and stride length.

Power Walk

Ref: Var.36   Impact Value   1.87

This is clearly the prime walk one would want to see in a pre-race parading horse. The latest buzz word describes it as a "panther" walk and is fairly apt. The topline of the neck, from the ears back to the saddle cloth, is carried at the horizontal or lower (blue line).

As shown in Picture 49 the front leg reaches out with a big extension (front yellow arrow) and although the picture doesn't show it, the hind leg comes way up under the body landing forward of, or equal to, where the front foot took off. This is referred to as an overstep and is depicted by the white arrow and circles. In the next phase of this horse's walk the white circled hind hoof should land along side, or in front of, the white circled front hoof at the arrowhead. Greater extension of the hind legs up under the body parlays into a longer stride by being able to drive from a more forward position. Extension and reach at the front

Chapter 8. Walking Styles

end, compliment the stride length also. A Power Walk horse has an appearance of flowing smoothly around the parade ring, giving one a sense of its willingness to move forward. It portrays a purposeful, business-like attitude as it powerfully stretches out.

The walk is a product of the shoulders and hips (red circles) and one can see the movement in these parts as the horse reaches and extends through the phases of this walk. Those exhibiting this walk generally stretch out well in a race. The walk gives the punter confidence that what has been observed pre-race can be replicated in race performance.

Walking Short

Ref: Var.37   Impact Value   0.86

This is the opposite of the Power Walk.

Compare the angle of the yellow arrow and the distance between the front feet (white arrow) of Picture 50, with the angles and distances in Picture 49.

There is not much extension in front and when one sees this walk it's almost like the shoulders are too tight and won't allow any reach to occur. There's usually no strong engagement from the hind legs, with small, stilted steps and the absence of an overstep (pink arrow). The blue arrow shows the elevated angle of the neck that is usually associated with a horse walking short.

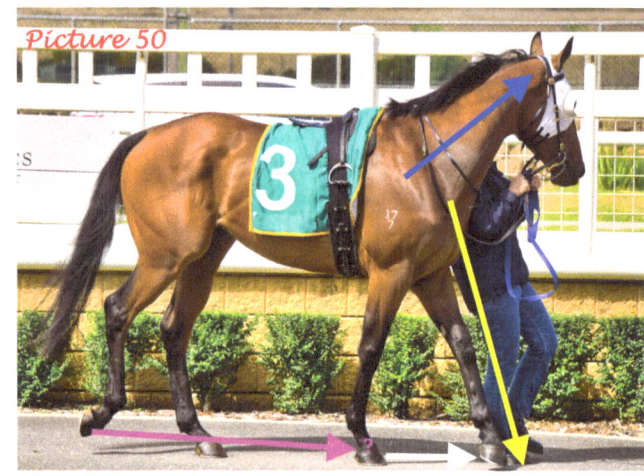

Jig Jogging

Ref: Var.38   Impact Value   0.87

This is a walking trait that one will see at nearly every yard. The horse is "up on its toes", dancing, bouncing, trotting on the spot almost. It's difficult to portray in a still photo, but the pink arrows show the diagonal feet leaving the ground and with the elevated neck one can sense the jogging occurring.

It can be a handful for the groom to control and is often associated with other negative factors and behavioural issues.

Chapter 8. Walking Styles

I've often heard the comment that a horse displaying this trait is "raring to go", but I've never subscribed to it, as the metrics suggest it's a negative and because of its association with other negative variables. The one exception is when it's combined with an arched neck and the Jig Jogging is very controlled and the animal is compliant with its handler. This is more of a sign of a horse "strutting its stuff" so to speak and feeling good about itself.

One other concession when marking Jig Jogging is to give them half a lap or so to settle down when they enter the parade ring Jig Jogging. They often Jig Jog in and then have a look around, relax and not do it again.

Double Tracking

Ref: Var.39   Impact Value   1.05

This is where the hindquarter is swung away from the handler (pink arrow) and the horse moves forward, usually at a jig jog, with the front legs and rear legs going down two different tracks (red arrows). The horse may also swing to the other side and do it too. The habit can continue after the rider mounts also.

The Impact Value implies that the trait is close to normal and neither a strong positive nor negative.

Scuffing

Ref: Var.40   Impact Value   0.22

This is a factor that won't be encountered frequently, but with its extremely low Impact Value, one would be very reluctant to consider the horse as a competitive chance.

It is identified by the noise the rear hooves make when they hit the ground. The horse seems very tight behind, with no extension of the step under the body and the hooves stab into the parade surface making a very audible scraping sound. Appears more in slow walking types that seem tired or lethargic but may be apparent in better walking types too.

Miscellaneous

There are three walk items here for which no metrics were obtained but they are worth a mention. The first one is the Stomper. Picture 53 shows the typical posture. It's unusual to see and may be an acquired habit or a sign the horse is annoyed. One of the front legs is flicked high out front and the hoof is stomped on the ground and after a few steps the action is repeated. I've seen horses do it for the entirety of the parade and others intermittently during the parade.

The second item is what I term "Hoof Echo". It's the sound a square landing hoof makes when on a hard, flat parade ring surface such as bitumen. I would liken it to the sound of tapping the open end of a plastic cup on a table and getting an echo sound.

Chapter 8. Walking Styles

It occurs when the horse is evenly landing the hoof, causing the whole shoe to touch at the same time. There's no scraping sound from uneven contact with the ground. It's very rhythmic and all four feet must be doing it. It's very distinct when you hear it and usually associated with a Power Walker. The horse is stepping out powerfully with clean, crisp hoof placement. Everything above the feet is in tune. It would be music to the ears of trainers who walk or trot up their horses in the afternoons for daily inspections, especially after gallop mornings.

I recall my second day of working for the syndicate out at a local track with the managers present, when a horse walked by and I impulsively tapped one manager's forearm and excitedly said twice, "Did you hear that?". He just turned and looked at me blankly. I told him I was referring to the sound the horse's walk made. There was no comment, he just stared at me with a puzzled look on his face. He wasn't a horse person, a figures expert, and this was obviously completely foreign to him and likely very odd.

I noticed him relating everything to the other manager, pointing and gesturing at horses' feet as they walked by, and a lot of shoulder shrugging and head shaking going on and I began to think I'd be looking for a new job the following week. I'd heard the sound before I'd looked at the horse's walk and reacted, but luckily the horse was a beautiful Power Walker and comfortably did the right thing for me in the race and I was still employed.

The final miscellaneous walking action is an odd one where the horse steps short on one side with a hind leg. The hoof doesn't advance beyond the opposite hoof in the step, it is basically just brought up alongside. Although it's not very common, it's extremely obvious, and even a complete novice observer would notice it. I've seen horses in Group One races do it and have just put it down to a habit or idiosyncrasy of the horse, as it never seems to affect their performance.

"At The Yard Checklist" – Walking Styles

Was the horse's neck carriage horizontal or lower?

Was the horse overstepping?

Was the horse extending out with front legs?

Did the walk give a sense of forward purpose and power?

Was it a Power Walk?

Did the horse appear to be taking small steps in front?

Were the rear steps small?

Was there an overstep?

What was the horse's neck angle? Elevated?

Was the horse Walking Short?

Was the horse "up on its toes", Jig Jogging?

Was the horse moving forward in a straight line or Double Tracking?

Was there an audible Scuffing sound from the hind hooves stabbing the ground?

Chapter 9. Behaviour

Of equal importance to assessing fitness of the racehorse is observation and appraisal of its demeanour and behaviour in the pre-race parade.

A horse in peak fitness may have its performance jeopardised by nervous or bad conduct on race day. Like any sport it's difficult for the physical side to function optimally if the mental side is compromised. So, it's imperative to consider, and be able to evaluate, race day conduct and ascertain how the horse is handling the experience.

In categorising the types of behaviours, the same positive and negative distinctions have been used with anything in between considered normal, average or acceptable behaviour. The positive behaviour category is Focus/Transition, and the negative behaviours consist of a variety of actions that constitute poor behaviour.

There is a myriad of triggers that can cause a horse to display substandard behaviour prior to a race. From a rough float trip to environmental factors, such as heat or strong winds. The cause is not something the pre-race analyst needs concern themselves with, only the capability to recognise the positive and negative demeanours.

Focus/Transition

Ref: Var.41   Impact Value   3.06

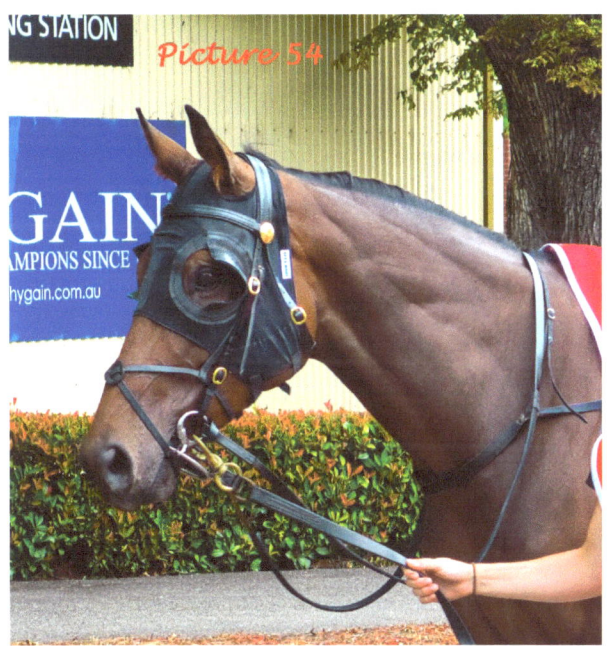

Identifying this factor requires astute observation and consistent practice from the horse watcher and even if one can only partly master it, the rewards are great. If you wanted to attend a race meeting and use only one factor for parade ring decisions, this would be it.

The aim is to identify a horse that is "in the zone". Most trainers can tell through a horse's attitude and demeanour when this transformation occurs. Everything they ask them to do is accepted with a business-like, sensible response. They are taken from their box, saddled up, mounted, exercised, washed, walked and fed all without any resistance or behaviour problems and with complete compliance. There's no problem for the rider or handlers, the horse cleans up its feed and is amenable to everything asked of it. The animal is responding positively and is in complete harmony with the stable routine and the trainer's exercise regime. It's "in the zone".

The task for the horse watcher is to see if we can identify these tuned in horses in the race day environment. I'll begin with the Focus part of the factor and work through a list of signals that provide insight for determining this positive factor.

   *Alert ears. As described in the head factors description. Pricked forward, no flickering or laying back.

 *Sharp eye with no rolling of them or white showing.
 *Good, consistent walk. No breaking into a jig jog or double tracking.
 *Neck carriage usually close to horizontal.
 *Usually quiet in the mouth. No bit chewing or salivating.
 *Loose or comfortable on the groom's lead strap.
 *Compliant when asked to stop by groom. No resistance.
 *If there is some sort of commotion in the ring with say another horse being difficult and unruly, the focused horse will remain calm, observe and continue when asked.
 *Common habit I've noticed is when the horse approaches the corner of a rectangular parade yard, they will often raise the head, prick the ears and look to the outside, and then round the corner, look back inside, and then drop the neck down to horizontal and walk on. They've had a look around, everything was OK, and they proceed unphased.
 *When the rider mounts, they stand quietly, there's no swinging the backside away, there's no dipping of the back when the jockey sits. Complete acceptance.
 *As they start to leave the yard and go onto the track, there is no jig jogging, head tossing, excitability etc. They are amenable to the jockey's commands just as they were with the groom.

It should be apparent from this list that what one is trying to identify is a horse that is completely comfortable with the race day environment, portrays a sense that he knows what is going on and is business-like in its approach to it all. Just like the habits and attitudes that the trainer has observed at the stable, the horse watcher has identified similar traits and attitudes at the mounting yard.

The racehorse passes through different stages on race day, and this is where the Transition side of the factor comes in. The process usually begins with a float trip, then on to the track stalls or tie ups, standing in the stalls, warm up walking in the pre-parade ring, saddling up, pre-parade ring walking again, pathway to main parade ring and then entering and parading in the main ring. All these changing environments have different levels of activity going on within them and can be a trigger for horses to begin to become nervous or apprehensive with the experience.

The watcher may not have access to all the areas mentioned but it is worthwhile to observe the horses' reactions to each change of area if possible. What one is looking for is no sudden change in behaviours as the horse moves from one section to the next. The focused horse will generally elevate the neck angle, prick the ears, have a good look around and then drop the head back down and continue to tractably walk the parade. They are virtually telling us "Yep, seen all this before, no problems, let's get on with it".

The strongest example of this factor in a major race that I've ever witnessed was Rekindling in Australia's great race, the 2017 Melbourne Cup. Horses in the race arrived on course three hours before the event and once I spotted him in the birdcage area, I couldn't take my eyes off him the whole time. Beside his beautiful flowing walk, he was the epitome of all the variables described here for a focused horse. His responsiveness to his handler, his attitude, everything just oozed confidence that he was there to run a race. You could almost hear the motor in him ticking over.

There won't be a lot of occurrences of the factor compared to some others, but with the strong metrics attached to it, one should really spend the time to accumulate the observation skills for it. I am always on the lookout for it, and I found that sometimes a parader just strikes you as a potential zoned in horse and warrants more intense scrutiny for verification of the factor.

Behaviour Negative

Ref: Var.42 Impact Value 0.76

This factor is comprised of a range of variables and carries a reasonably low Impact Value as one would expect. Poor behaviour correlates with poor performance and these badly behaved horses are generally

Chapter 9. Behaviour

not in the correct mental state for optimal performance. However, there are horses that are just plain difficult and may display bad behavioural traits every time, and one may become familiar with their antics after seeing it many times, but regardless of performance results, these horses were still assessed as negative behaviour.

One of the most important, and frequently marked in this category, is Rider Resentment. Observation of the horse as the jockey approaches to be legged up is where signs become evident. It may be a subtle laying back of the ears, to swinging the backside away and clearly trying to avoid the rider getting on board. This can escalate into scattering other horses in the yard and on some occasions it's almost as if the jockey needs to break the horse in before getting it onto the track! Other signs are dipping the back as the rider lands in the saddle and trying to run off on the groom and rider.

Difficulty for the groom is a common variable seen also. The horse is completely non-compliant to the groom's commands, trying to charge forward on the lead strap with the groom virtually getting towed along, or pushing the groom into the fences, or just strong unruly behaviour that's clearly difficult for the handler. Often horses doing this type of thing are brought into the centre of the yard and circled around almost like a longing session and this was also considered as negative behaviour.

Refusal is a trait that falls into bad behaviour too. This is when a horse stubbornly refuses to enter the mounting yard or more often, go out onto the track. They just plant all four feet and let everyone know they're not going anywhere. This is seen at the barriers too. The situation usually has the groom pulling hard on the lead up front and a handful of helpers waving arms and urging the horse on from behind.

Time into the parade area is included under negative behaviour also. Sometimes, by arrangement with officials, a horse might be given permission to go out to the barriers without parading, before all the other horses and sometimes they may be held back until the others have left. These horses are generally whisked through quickly denying the watcher a proper viewing. Even though the tactic may prove successful in the race result, I still considered it a behavioural deficiency and judge it as a negative.

Other variables of this factor may include kicking out behind, aggression towards other horses, shying away from things, bumping into a rail or fence, dumping a rider, or any actions that may be considered away from sensible or normal behaviour.

Those regular meeting attendees who may be interested in collecting their own information for a personal database may want to break this factor up into individual categories of the variables mentioned here, for further accuracy. My personal choice was to generalise them into one category.

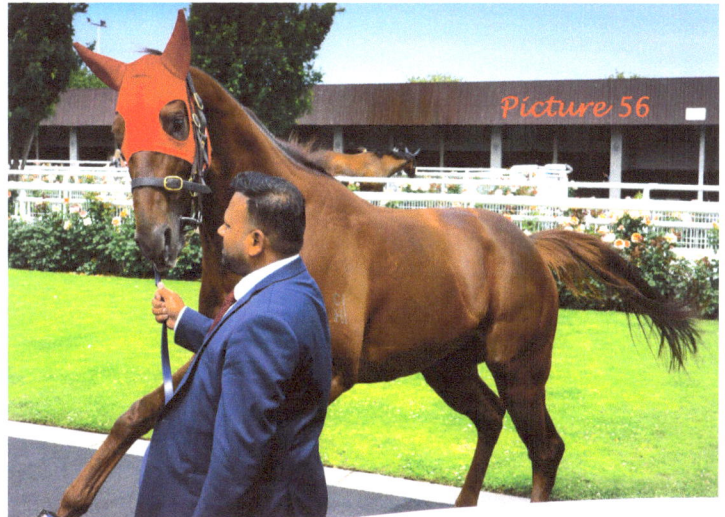

Chapter 9. Behaviour

"At The Yard Checklist" – Behaviour

Was the horse alert? Positive ears?

Was the horse walking sensibly?

Was the neck carriage low?

Was the mouth relatively still?

Was the horse compliant with the handler's commands? Was the horse comfortably loose on the lead strap?

Was the horse responsively calm to any distractions?

Did the horse have a good look around when entering the parade ring and appear unphased?

Was the horse completely accepting of the rider mounting?

Was there any sign of excitability as the horse left the ring for the track?

Could the horse be considered as a yes for Focus/Transition factor?

Was there any sign of rider resentment? Negative ears, swinging away, dipping of the back, refusal to stand for rider to mount?

Was the groom experiencing difficulty controlling the horse?

Was the horse circled in the middle of the yard?

Did the horse refuse to move at any stage?

Was the horse presented early or late into the parade ring?

Did the horse kick out behind, shy, dump the rider, bump a fence or rail?

Chapter 10. Coat

The coat of a horse is the most common thing people notice or refer to when looking at a parading racehorse. The coat gives an insight into the general health of the animal and the metrics support this with good numbers for positive coats and low numbers for poor coat conditions.

During winter it's a natural occurrence for coats to grow longer and woollier as protection against the elements. Some stables clip or partially clip winter coats. Full winter coats create a couple of items that the yard watcher must deal with. Firstly, they are never as shiny as a summer coat and a closer observation is required prior to deeming one as dull. Secondly, it's been mentioned to me that some have difficulty with fitness assessments, as the longer coat inhibits them seeing the muscle definitions. With practice and experience one can look through the coat and still be able to judge the muscle development. Also, horses may vary in the time they take to shed their winter coat and coming out of winter it may be common to see a field of horses parading with coats ranging from long and woolly still to glossy spring coats. I've never collected information on whether horses with slow dropping winter coats are disadvantaged at all.

The three coat categories are Glowing, Dapple and Dull.

Glowing Coat

Ref: Var.43   Impact Value   1.46

A shine on a horse's coat is due to the reflection of light on it and a dull coat absorbs the light and hence, no reflection.

Trainers are very good carers of their animals, and most racehorses will have some level of sheen or glow to their coat. When marking this factor, I looked for the exceptional glowing coats and just as importantly those with a rich deep colour to them as appears in Picture 57. There are feed supplements, such as vegetable oil, that will enhance the shine of a horse's coat enormously, and subsequently, I would tend to look at the depth of colour and texture of the coat. The texture of a healthy, gleaming coat should also have a fine, silky appearance, with the hairs laying very flat. Even on dull overcast days when there is not much light reflection possible, the texture of the coat will enable you to judge its condition.

A gleaming, rich coloured, silky coat is a good sign of the level of health of the animal and an indication of its response to, and acquisition from, its feed, training and care regimen. This is borne out by the metric returned of a 1.46 Impact Value.

Dappled Coat

Ref: Var.44   Impact Value   1.32

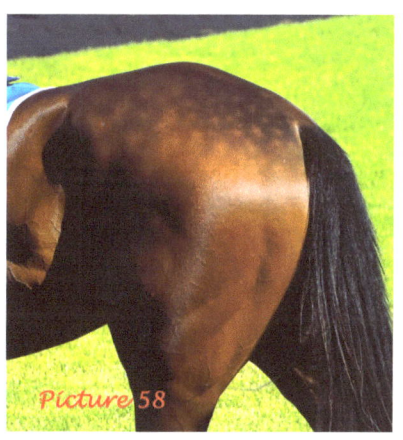

Another sign of a healthy horse is the appearance of dapples in the coat. They can present all over the body as lighter shade spots as shown in Picture 58. They occur due to variations in pigmentation

Chapter 10. Coat

in the hair. Once again, like a shiny coat, they are the product of the horse's positive response to the nutrition, care and training program it's received and is also reflected in the solid Impact Value metric.

Dull Coat

Ref: Var.45   Impact Value   0.68

Picture 59

This is the opposite of a shiny or dappled coat and may indicate to the yard analyst that the horse may be struggling to thrive through its racing and training program. The coat is absorbing light and not reflecting it and appears very dry and rough looking. The hair may seem to stand up more as opposed to the flat silky appearance of a glowing coat.

When assessing dull coats towards the end of winter, concessions should be made for those horses that are shedding their winter coats, as these can look very dull and long. It's just a natural process that they go through, with some shedding quicker than others, and they shouldn't be penalised for it. In the warmer weather months when there are an abundance of horses parading with a sheen on their coats it's not difficult to spot a coat that is failing to show any lustre, and this is how the metrics were gathered for the factor. The very poor Impact Value exemplifies the importance of noting the factor.

"At The Yard Checklist" – Coat

Was the coat glowing?

Was the colour deep and rich?

Did the hair appear silky and was it lying flat?

Were there dapples apparent?

Was the coat not reflecting light and slightly standing?

Chapter 11. Sweating

Sweating is a component of a horse's cooling system and can be observed in the pre-race parade due to a variety of environmental and physical conditions.

The primary cause of sweating in the racehorse is the ambient temperature and humidity of the prevailing race day conditions. Higher temperatures and humidity will obviously result in a horse presenting with sweat, and the percentage of the field that do show some form of sweating can provide an insight into the normality of it for the particular conditions. Often on very hot and humid days, 100% of the field will be sweating, but it is the extent of the sweating that the yard analyst can evaluate. On the flip side, when cooler and milder weather conditions prevail, and a horse is noticed with some sweat, and no other horse is sweating, then that's when alarm bells should go off. That horse is in opposition to what the rest of the participants are implicating is normal for the weather. Some other factor is at play.

Nerves, apprehension and agitation are other triggers of sweating. Just as they cause humans to sweat, horses likely react similarly. Those affected by these factors normally sweat in conjunction with other factors that have been described earlier, such as, jig jogging, head tossing, bit chewing and negative behavioural attributes. The combination of the nerves and the physical activity produces the sweating.

Other causes of sweating may be due to friction from the gear on the horse. The saddle, saddlecloth, girth, bridle, breastplate etc. It's perfectly normal for these areas to get warmer and show some dampness even in colder conditions. Also, on a sunny spring day you may encounter a horse that hasn't fully shed its winter coat, and this causes them to sweat somewhat. As long it's only wet hair and not excessively dripping I would tend to not penalise it as a negative sweater.

So, when marking the sweat categories in the parade, one should be considering the weather conditions on the day, and the degrees of the sweating, how excessive it is.

Bum Sweat

Ref: Var.46   Impact Value   1.14

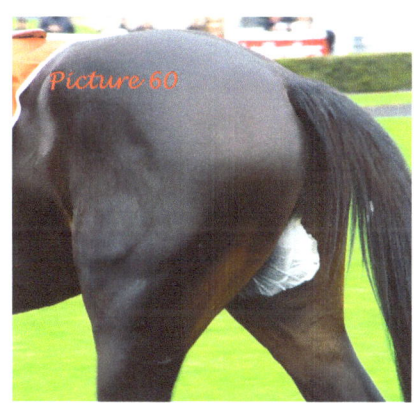

Often referred to as kidney sweat, this occurs between the upper hind legs, and presents as a white lather, which is easily noticeable and very common.

The one stipulation when this was marked is that it hadn't broken and started to run down the inner leg. As long as the lather held its position it was included in the category, and as the Impact Value shows, it is not considered a negative sweat when contained to those parameters and is a slight positive attribute.

Body Sweat

Ref: Var.47   Impact Value   0.85

In this category, any body part that was showing sweat was included in the marking. Even if it was obvious that very hot and humid weather was causing all horses to sweat profusely, it was still included as it can be used as a reference to look back on when trying to understand the cause of a poor performance. Not all horses may handle the conditions the same.

Picture 61 shows a horse with a flank sweat occurring in mild weather conditions. This may occur on the neck, shoulder, rump or any part of the anatomy and should be noted accordingly. The sweating in the

Chapter 11. Sweating

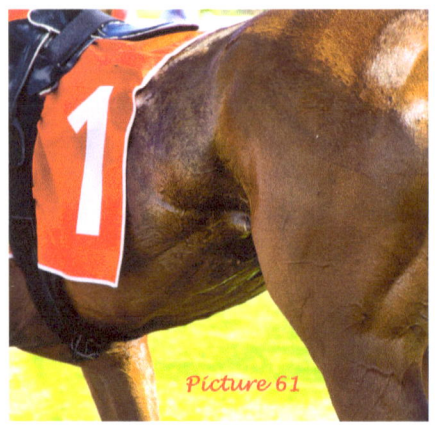

Picture 61

picture is very light and it can be seen a lot heavier at times, to the point where it is dripping on the ground.

Included here is the negative extension of the previous category of Bum Sweat. This is where the lather has become excessive, broken from its hold, and started to run down the leg and even drip to the ground. In this circumstance often the white lather can disappear and the excessive sweating results in a clear watery trickle down the leg, being less noticeable than the obvious white lather.

One concession made here is when some moisture or small lather caused by friction from gear on the horse, such as a girth or saddlecloth, is apparent. If it wasn't excessive and running heavily down away from the cause it was overlooked, and not included in the data collection.

In this variable, all the body sweats, no matter what level they were at, from profuse to light, were lumped together. Generally, there is similarity in the degree of sweating across the whole field, relevant to the prevailing conditions. However, the yard watcher may possibly add more weight to their decisions on horses that go against what most of the field are doing. If most of the horses are sweating to a moderate level and one is excessively running like a tap, then that is a noted difference. Alternatively, if one is not sweating at all, then that may mean it is handling the situation better than most.

Picture 62

So, when assessing the sweating of horses in the parade ring we are looking for indications outside the norm. Heavy sweating compared to light sweating, patchy neck or flank sweating in mild conditions or sweating associated with behavioural problems are a few examples. If a horse one is interested in investing in is sweating under conditions that seem reasonable to do so in, then that shouldn't be a deterrent to discarding the selection. Sweating is quite natural in certain conditions, and with experience and close observation, sensible decisions can be made as to the evaluation of the negativity of the sweat the horse watcher has observed.

Picture 62 shows a neck sweater and Picture 63 depicts a heavy full body sweater.

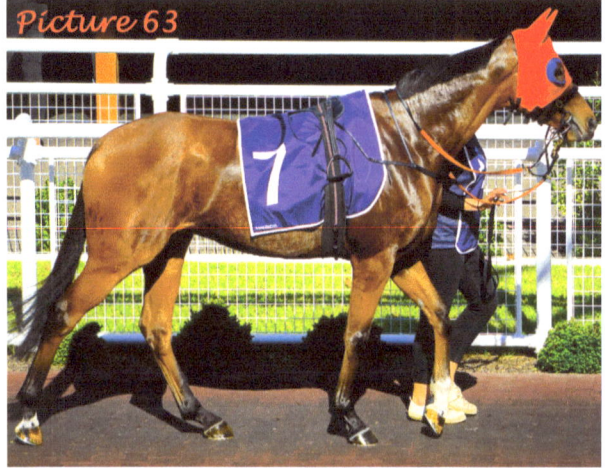

Picture 63

Chapter 11. Sweating

<u>"At The Yard Checklist" – Sweat</u>

What are the prevailing weather conditions?

Are the horses generally sweating to a level one would expect from those conditions?

Was the horse sweating excessively?

Was the horse not sweating at all?

Did the horse have Bum Sweat?

Was it running down the leg?

Was the horse sweating on the flank?

Was it sweating on the neck or other areas?

Was there heavy sweat running away or dripping from any of the horse's gear?

Were conditions cool to mild and some Body Sweat was evident?

Chapter 12. Size

The size referred to in the marking of this variable is height. Big and small, not how lean, muscular or robust a horse appeared. Decisions on categorising a horse as either big or small required that it be a standout in the parading group for that race. Occasionally this may have meant that multiple horses were included in each category but, if there is a clear size distinction from the bulk of the field, that is fine. If there is uncertainty in determining or measuring size across a field of parading horses a helpful method is to use some sort of background structure, such as a fence rail, as a yardstick to compare each horse as they parade past.

There is an often spoken about relationship between horse size and track configuration. Bigger horses may prefer larger, roomier tracks with less turns and smaller horses may have an advantage on smaller tighter turning courses. In my racing jurisdiction, both types of tracks are prevalent and from looking at the relatively small data sample collected, the Impact Values didn't seem to vary much. The same lack of Impact Value variation held true when the correlation between size and track going was looked at. A further examination with a larger data sample may shed more light on these relationships, but personally I feel it could be an individual horse thing and study of a horse's form history and past performances may be a solid guide.

The Impact Values from the data expose an overall bias or advantage towards the bigger horse, but I suspect that there may be cause for an element of the adage "horses for courses" at play here.

Big

Ref: Var.48   Impact Value   1.13

Small

Ref: Var.49   Impact Value   0.88

"At The Yard Checklist" – Size

Was the horse compared against a background structure?

Was the horse clearly bigger than the majority of the field?

Was the horse clearly smaller than most of the field?

Chapter 13. Droppings

Observing the droppings of a horse may seem strange, or even amusing to some, but the Impact Values suggest it is a practice well worthy of being noted. Two categories were detailed here, Loose and Firm, and the distinction between them is based on the consistency and colour of the droppings.

Over the course of years of parade watching and becoming familiar with different stables and the pre-race presentation of their horses, one can accurately predict what the droppings will be like. It's clear they have a preferred feed and supplementation program leading into a race, which in turn leads to the consistent appearance of their droppings. I haven't kept data to verify this, but my experience tells me that this is something highly associated with the more successful stables too, and the droppings tend to be in the Loose category.

Another observation is that staying horses don't seem to drop as much as the shorter distance horses. Whether it's due to the style of training they do, more long aerobic work, or their feeding regime, and that tends to clean them out, I'm not sure, but it's not uncommon for a full field of stayers to leave the parade ring clear of any droppings.

Scouring is basically the human diarrhea equivalent and is not often encountered in the parade ring. Occasionally there may be an obvious, very nervous, edgy horse that is spurting watery droppings, with it getting caught in the tail and running down the leg. The animal has clearly worked itself into a terrible state and is one to be avoided investment wise.

Loose

Ref: Var.50   Impact Value   1.7

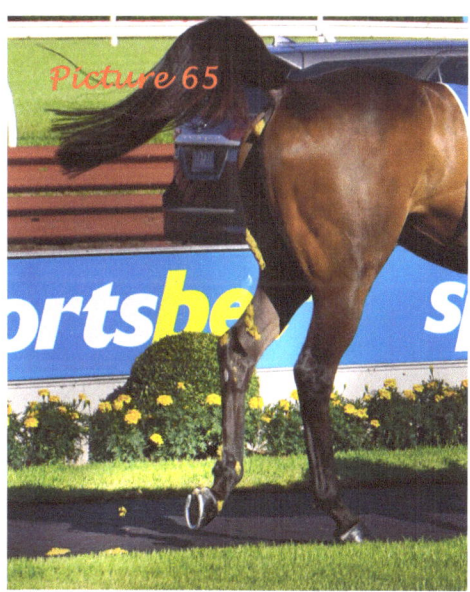

Picture 64 illustrates Loose droppings. It is usually defined by a trail of small flat droppings, released as the horse walks along. If the horse releases when stationary it will still be fairly flat because of its liquid makeup.

Due to its watery consistency, it doesn't pile up and is generally pale in colour. The looseness of it is quite normal and as the strong Impact Value suggests it is a very positive variable.

Picture 65 is an "action shot", so to speak, of the occurrence.

Firm

Ref: Var.51   Impact Value   0.88

As seen in the accompanying pictures, Firm droppings have less liquid content and hence tend to pile up more. They are often a darker colour than the paler Loose droppings, but both can be a green colour if the horses are being fed lucerne hay or chaff. Colour is a product of the differing hays and chaff they are being fed and it's the consistency of the droppings that is most important. One thing you don't want to see, and I have seen it a couple of times, is when the consistency is like dry pebbles. It may indicate an electrolyte/dehydration problem and not a good sign for an animal going into a competitive event.

Even though the Impact Value is slightly below the normal for the population and returns a big gap compared to Loose droppings, it shouldn't be considered abnormal or a negative. No trainer is going to be concerned over firm droppings, it may just come down to the differing pre-race regimes that stables employ that cause the discrepancy in Impact Values.

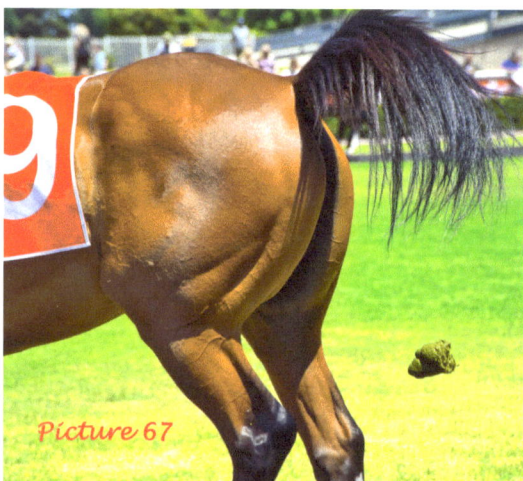

"At The Yard Checklist" – Droppings

What was the consistency of the droppings?

Were they very moist?

Were they trailed out in a series of small flat circles?

Or was there a larger, flat, moist presentation?

Were the droppings drier with a tendency to pile up more?

Was the horse agitated, nervous, jig jogging and spurting watery droppings, getting caught in the tail and running down the leg?

Chapter 14. Grooms

In marking this category, I only went with the negative groom and not the with the positive side. A lot of the time grooms are deemed positive because the horse is allowing them to be. Purely through the horses' compliance and good behaviour the groom, or strapper as they're referred to here in Australia, can let the horse comfortably walk a parade. On the flip side a strapper may do a great job of controlling an unruly horse. In both these instances the situation seems to be governed more by the horse than the groom and should probably be marked for horse factors rather than groom factors. That is why I looked for negative groom habits as they are directly affecting the horse, not initiated by the horse.

Good strappers/grooms know their horses and go with them. First thing they'll do is try to be leading it on a nice loose lead strap. They remain very calm, and their horses respond. There is no sharp jagging on the lead rope just polite corrections. Granted a lot depends on the horse's behaviour but even with unruly, pushy horses, there's no anger displays, they'll just lean the shoulder into the horse and do their best.

A case in point here is the groom pictured with the horse in the Twisted Neck category.(Picture 17). A very experienced groom who knows that the horse likes to carry his head that way and simply goes with him. Too often with that type of head and neck carriage grooms continually try to straighten and correct them, which can end up in a tussle and set the horse on a negative attitude path. Similarly with the Ground Licker picture. (Picture 19).You can see the groom is letting the horse do it and not trying to force its head up causing unnecessary bit pressure in the mouth that may result in resentment. Both those traits rank very highly and should be encouraged and not have attempts to correct them.

Groom Negative

Ref: Var.52   Impact Value   0.78

There are two main actions that would cause a groom to be marked as negative. The first is what I termed a "jagger". This is where the groom continually pulls the lead strap, causing pressure on the bit in the horse's mouth. It's very common, and I'm not even sure some grooms know they're doing it. Even when the horse is a dream to handle you can see the strapper jag, jag, jagging on the horse's mouth. It's a bad habit. When the horse reacts by lifting its head, its usually more, and stronger jagging from the groom. Numerous times I've witnessed this situation escalate to the point where there is a complete behaviour change from the horse and a breakout of body sweat as it leaves the parade ring.

The second instance seems to arise from the latest trend of grooms reaching over the neck to grab the right rein and have the lead strap in their left hand only. It seems to be the go-to position for some, even though the horse is obviously easy to handle. One can sense that it is done by some who are fearful of getting their feet stood on, as they tend to angle their upper body in towards the horse and their feet well away. I'm sure it has its place and is well done most of the time, but I have noticed it can lead to similar problems as described for the jagger. Because the groom controls the right rein, any time the horse wants to look left, turn its head to the left or even ground lick, there seems to be a necessity to correct with a pull on the rein. Restricting these natural, innocent moves often leads to a tugging to and fro, and an eventual upsetting of the horse, particularly the mental state. The situation may have gone from a horse that wanted to parade around the ring having a look at things in a reasonable manner to one where it has spent the whole parade having the bit tugged in its mouth. Not the optimum pre-race scenario.

Another occurrence that would constitute a negative marking is when a horse enters the mounting yard and is immediately taken into the centre by the groom and spun around them in circles without any attempt to participate in the parade with the other horses and be given a chance to settle down. Fair enough if the horse has done some laps, proved too unruly and is taken to the centre and circled as a best control method. I think that when a groom goes straight to the centre and circles, it's more a sign of a lack

Chapter 14. Grooms

of confidence from the groom in their handling ability rather than a need of the horse. I've certainly never seen this practice calm a horse down, usually the opposite.

Other instances of groom negativity may be aggressive handling of the horse, in the form of a slap behind with the end of the lead rope, severe jags on the mouth or even an elbow to the ribs as I've seen. Usually borne out of a groom's anger and frustration from trying to handle a difficult horse.

"At The Yard Checklist" – Grooms

Was the handler allowing the horse to be itself?

Was the groom maintaining a calm attitude?

Was the groom continually jagging on the lead strap?

Was the groom pulling on the outside rein every time the horse wanted to move its head?

Was the horse immediately asked to circle in the centre after entering the ring?

Was the horse given the opportunity to parade and settle down before circling in the centre?

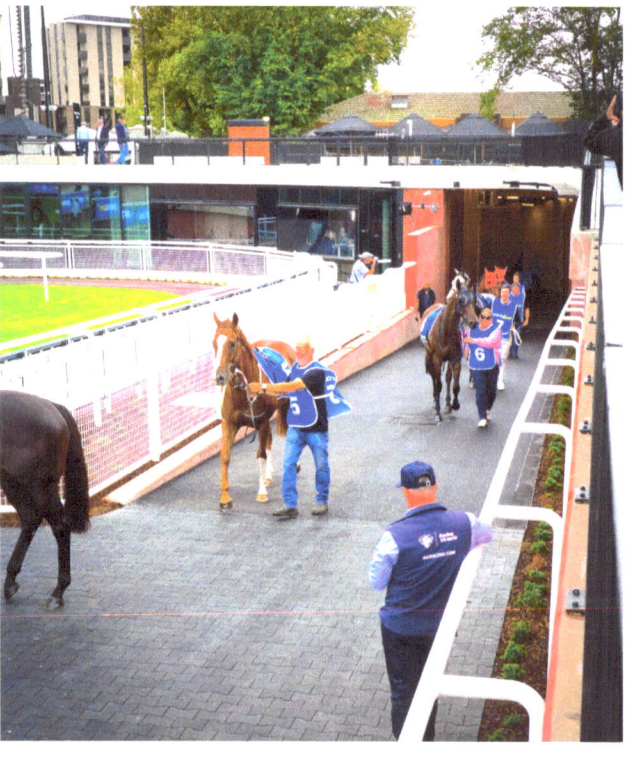

Chapter 15. Canter Off

The Canter Off factor is when the horse goes onto the track and warms up on the way to the barrier. Both positive and negative assessments were recorded, with the profile required for the positive side returning some of the strongest figures of all the horse factors.

Not all horses get the opportunity to exhibit "Canter Off Positive" as they may only trot to the barriers, get led by the clerk of the course or lead ponies.

Assessing a racehorse's journey to the gates is a very important tool in determining how it may perform. It's commonly an extension of factors identified from the parade ring and very predictive of a horse's tractability in a race. An example is the following two very frequently observed scenarios.

The jig jogging head tosser, that rushes out onto the track, fighting the rider who is attempting to settle it, (How would the respiratory pattern be?), loads into the gates in a fair sweat, jumps, throws the head and over-races. In comparison is the relaxed walking still mouth, who calmly accepts the rider mounting, heads out onto the track without rushing, completely compliant with the rider's commands and canters off happily to the gates, loads, jumps and travels comfortably in the race.

Racetracks provide two environments (possibly three, if access to the stalls area is available) for the horse watcher to assess the horses, the parade ring and on the track on the way to the gates. So often the things we identify in these two areas correlate with performance in the race.

Canter Off Positive

Ref: Var.53   Impact Value   2.1

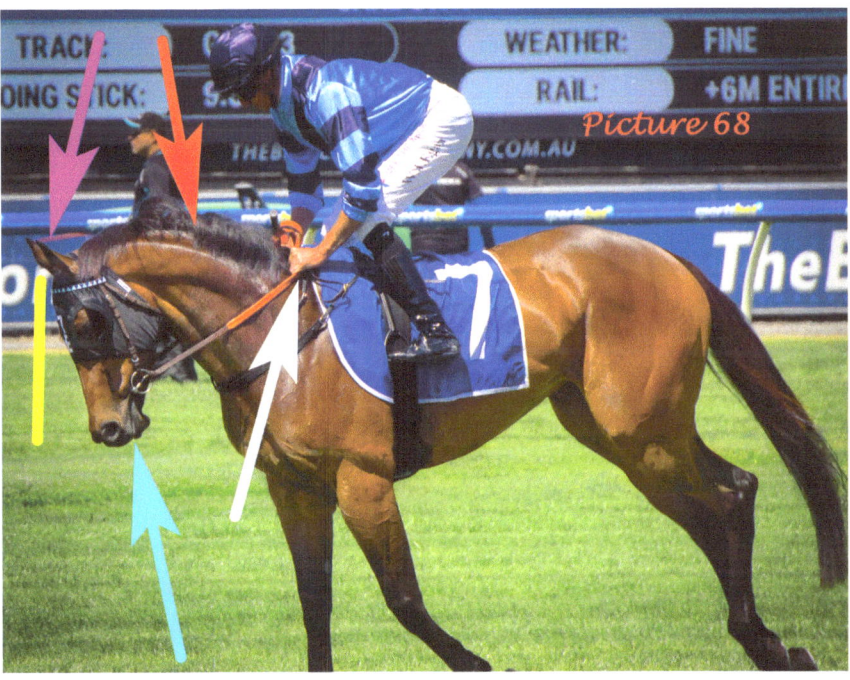

Picture 68

With such a strong Impact Value, it's imperative that the analyst has this factor in their box of tools. With experience, through practice and close observation, identification of the required profile is not that difficult.

Firstly, the top of the neckline, or along the mane, (red arrow) can be straight or arched, as in this picture, and the closer to horizontal the neck carriage is the better. The profile of the forehead, from between the ears to between the nostrils should be around the vertical. (Yellow line). It's slightly behind the vertical in the picture. The ears should be alert and pointing forward (pink arrows) and the mouth should be closed and static. (Blue arrows). There should be no opening and closing of the mouth. The jockey's hands are planted on the base of the horse's neck and stay there. Rein length is set from bit to hands and the horse should maintain the profile through it's warm up to the gates. The jockey is comfortably perched on top as the picture shows.

The more you look at this factor, you'll notice that a lot of horses immediately just slot straight into the profile after the rider asks for a canter and maintain it all the way to the barriers. It's a display of comfort from the horse, in both his physical and mental state.

Canter Off Negative

Ref: Var.54   Impact Value   0.49

The vast difference between the values of the negative and positive metrics of this factor exemplifies its importance.

These are the actions that constituted marking a negative canter off.

    *Rushing onto the track with the rider having difficulty restraining the horse.
    *Reluctance or refusal to go out onto the track. Baulking, spinning around.
    *Refusal to turn around. Horses often walk or trot in one direction down the track, then turn and canter off to the gates. Some will refuse to turn and go and prove very difficult for the jockey.
    *Refusal to move. I've seen this quite a few times. The horse steps onto the track and becomes a statue. Usually a crowd quickly gathers, with everyone urging on the horse. Often ends with the horse moving off when they've decided they're good and ready.
    *Head bobbing at the trot off. This is where the head lifts as the hoof hits the ground, indicating there may be a soreness or lameness issue in that particular leg. Identification of it is probably for the experienced horse person, but you do see it, and a work colleague of mine was extremely accurate at picking it.
    *Head tossing, reefing and pulling on the reins. Generally unruly and causing obvious difficulty for the rider. If this action is only mild initially, I would allow 50-100 metres to see if it continues as the jockeys are very good at settling them down.
    *Violently flicking their tail around as they're cantered off.
    *Too fast. The horse wants to fly around to the gates. The jockey's lower leg will be angled forward in the irons, the upper body leaning back, and the hands will be lifted trying to restrain the horse.
    *Any other incident due to attitude or bad behaviour from the horse. Brushing a rail, tossing a rider etc.

Chapter 15. Canter Off

"At The Yard Checklist" – Canter Off

Did the horse calmly go out onto the track?

Or did it baulk, spin around, refuse?

Did it try to rush out onto the track with the rider trying to control it?

Was it obedient to the rider's walk, trot and canter commands or, head toss and become difficult to handle?

Was there a discernible head bob when trotting off?

Was it thrashing its tail around repeatedly?

Did the horse just slot in to the "positive profile" and maintain it to the barriers?

Was the horse accompanied by a clerk of course or lead pony?

Was the horse trying to go too fast on the rider?

Did any other incident occur, caused by the horse?

Chapter 16. Behind The Gates

With the advent of modern betting platforms and the availability of on course big screen vision and off course vision streams, bet placement has become viable right down close to jump time. This has also provided the horse watcher with the opportunity to obtain a complete profile of a horse, from stall to starting gates.

The horses have left the parade ring/crowd environment, stretched their legs on the way to gates and are then circled by the riders behind the gates awaiting loading. Prior to a punter making a final investment decision they can check for any change in the horse this procedure may have initiated. Be it positive, negative or no change. As an example, the horse that might have been deemed slightly edgy in the parade may now be circling behind the barriers, very comfortably on a loose rein for the rider and walk straight into the gates. Alternatively, the same edgy horse may now be sweating profusely, tossing its head, with the rider gripped up tight on it and being difficult to load into the barriers.

Identification of demeanour changes at this stage of the race day process can enable one to "sign off" on a wagering decision. Some of the factors to look for and take on board follow.

> Does the horse's demeanour correlate to its parade ring demeanour?
> Is it circling compliantly on a loose rein for the rider?
> Is it dropping its neck to a near horizontal position?
> Does it lead up and walk into the stalls calmly?
> Does it stand quietly in the gates?
> Does it circle tossing its head with the rider having to strongly restrain?
> Has it turned into a muck lather of sweat?
> Was it refusing to be led up towards the gates?
> Was it proving reluctant to enter the stalls? Turning side on or kicking out.
> Was it very unsettled in the gates?
> Was there an incident?
> Was it vet checked?

As with each differing environment the racehorse must go through on race day, what the analyst is trying to observe, when the horse is at its final destination of the procedure, is any change of disposition and take the findings on board for a wagering decision. It's not uncommon for circumstances to change, from parade ring to starting gates and it's probably wise for the punter to have that final check if the situation allows.

Chapter 17. Post Race

No metrics were collected for the various post-race variables we can look at to ascertain an insight into how the horse may have been affected by the race, but it is a great opportunity to conduct some quality control on oneself. It's subject to one having access to see the horses return to scale, but if they can be seen, one can measure the accuracy of their pre-race fitness assumptions, by identification of some post-race factors.

Firstly, how strong was the horse pulling up after the post? Was the jockey having a hard time slowing it down or did it pull up primarily, of its own accord, shortly after the post? The answer is a horse with more to give and one that was well and truly affected by the exertion. Did those scenarios correspond with the pre-race fitness expectations?

All horses will naturally be breathing heavily after the physical demands of a race, some more than others. Signs to look for are, a louder breathing noise compared to others, large heaving movement of the ribcage and strong expansion and flaring of the nostrils. Keep in mind that environmental elements, such as temperature and humidity, may cause an elevation in breathing intensity. Important if one is monitoring recoveries on a race-to-race basis. An excessive blow compared to a previous race, when the expectation is that the horse should be fitter, could be due to the environmental conditions.

The fit horses will show themselves by being a lot quieter in their breathing, having quicker recoveries and generally little agitation when being unsaddled and handled.

"Blowing up over the rump", as it is often referred to, is evident post-race in a horse that may be lacking in fitness. It is due to the accumulation of lactic acid in the rump muscles that causes them to "blow up".

In Picture 72 this winner was displaying very mild symptoms of it. The rump muscles raise up (pink arches), which causes a channel down the spine.

It's easily identifiable and is another variable for the horse watcher to look for post-race in assessing current race fitness and any improvement to come.

My interpretation of the posture of a horse that is "feeling it" after its race is, an elevated tail, a lowered neck with the head and nostrils reaching forward gasping for air. There's a big deficit going on and when being unsaddled, they tend to fidget on their feet, often try and reverse away, or kick out with a hind leg. They're not enamoured with the standing still and are keen to get on the move.

It's a very worthwhile practice to watch and assess the horses as they return to the paddock. Some rewarding feedback can be gleaned on the accuracy of pre-race assessments and even information for a horse's future race assignments.

Chapter 18. Stalls

Just as the post-race checks can provide insight into one's assessments, attending the stalls area pre-race, can offer a good opportunity to observe things that others may not see or know about. A lot takes place there and it's worthwhile to take the time to attend and be aware of what to look for. That's provided access is available to the stall areas, as not all tracks I attend allow the public in.

It's especially advantageous if you've come to the races to wager on a horse or horses, that your form analysis has led you to believe, are strong propositions. Armed with the knowledge of what to look for, you can follow the horse through its complete race day cycle and determine if its physicality and demeanour equate to the strength of the form analysis. All these titbits of information, from stall to parade ring, combine to develop a profile of a horse to assist in your investment decisions.

No metrics were collected for the stall area factors, but the descriptions that follow are sound principles to look for.

The first encounter may be to see a horse arrive in the stall area. Or even see them come off their transport. If they're not wearing a rug we can check to see if the travel has caused them to sweat. Have they arrived in a muck lather, or are they dry and very calm? How is their behaviour?

The next opportunity is when they're in the tie ups. This is a good time to observe their eye sharpness and facial features. Do their facial expressions relate comfort, or discomfort with their situation? Have they been accompanied by a companion pony? If so, is this usual, or a first-time occurrence?

How is their behaviour in the tie ups? Are they kicking out behind? Pawing the ground? Throwing their head up and down? Shuffling and fidgeting with their feet? Or are they "standing square"? Front feet evenly standing, with no pointing of a toe from one hoof, or is there continual changing of weight bearing from one side to the other?

When the horse is taken out for a walk, it is a chance to assess fitness without the saddle and saddlecloth on. How is its behaviour? How much walking has it been given? Did it get stirred up easily, or did it take it calmly in its stride?

In Australia the horses are saddled up in the stalls and then walked to the parade ring, so on most occasions watchers don't get the chance to see how the horse reacted to the process. In a lot of overseas jurisdictions, they are taken to stalls adjacent to the parade ring for saddling and that provides the chance to see the horse's acceptance or not of the process.

Most of the factors that have been described previously, both physical and demeanour related, can be assessed in this area too. My optimum profile of an early look at a horse in the stalls area is one that walks in inquisitively but sensibly, taking everything in, with alert ears, no sweat from the travel and compliant with the grooms demands. Stands square in the tie ups and behaves well when taken for a walk and saddled.

Chapter 19. Bandages

The presence of bandages on a horse requires the observer to interpret the possible reasons for applying them and whether it is a concern or not. A determination must be made if they are standard gear for the horse, preferred by the stable on all horses, or are applied over an injury or problem spot. In a lot of racing jurisdictions, it's almost standard fare for bandages such as tendon wraps (Picture 73) to be applied. They are there for precautionary support and not because of injury.

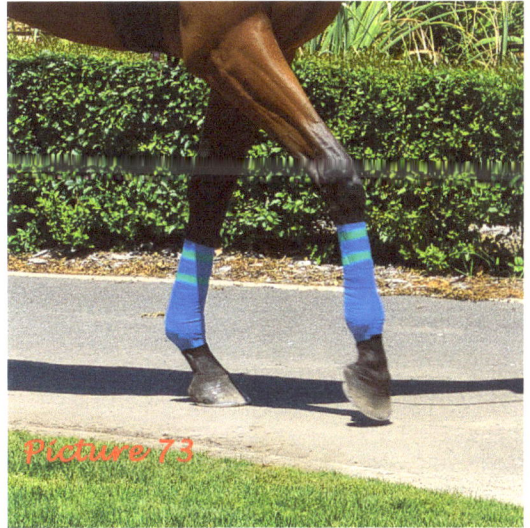

Picture 73

There are instances when the application of bandages should spark our attention. If a horse we're familiar with parades with a bandage for the first time, it may indicate there's been an issue between races. Similarly, a bandage on one leg only may provoke caution and the higher up the leg it is applied, further caution.

There are a few problems that can evolve from a horse's galloping action that may cause injury to itself and hence prompt the necessity for bandaging and lead to a possible reluctance of the horse to stretch out properly at the gallop, for fear of hurting itself again. Bumper bandages, or rear fetlock tapes (Picture 74), are one of the more common examples that are seen. The rear of the fetlock strikes the ground causing bruising and grazing of the skin in the area. "Speedy cutting" as it is termed, is where the opposite foot hits the inside of the leg around the knee area. "Scalping" occurs when the rear hoof gets hit by the toe of the front foot. "Overreaching" is caused by the hind hoof striking the lower leg or heel area of the front leg.

These issues may be the reason for a horse having a bandage in the corresponding areas that these problems occur. It's very much something to consider pre-race, as there is the possibility it may affect the horse again during the race and instil a reluctance to stride fully, resulting in below par performance.

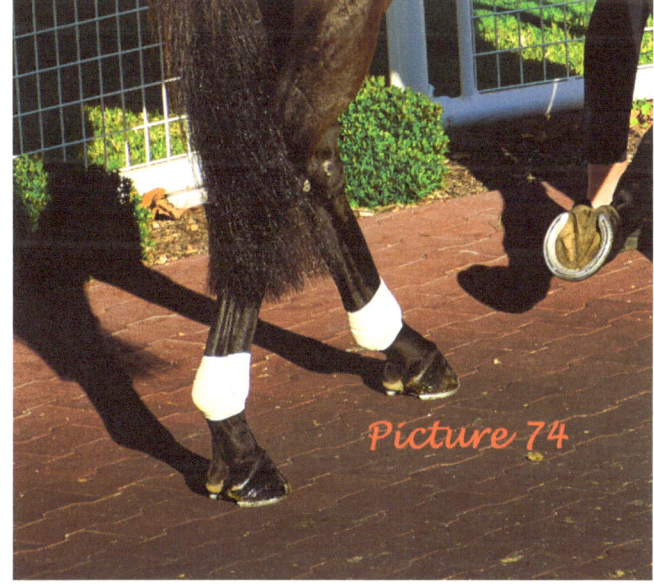

Picture 74

Another aspect to knowing about these galloping action problems is in the post-race situation where one may be looking for answers for poor performances. Many a time I've been looking over the horses as they return to the mounting yard and noticed various lower leg cuts and abrasions. From "knife slice" type cuts on the inside below the knees, to chunks removed from the bulb of the heel to the abraded fetlock bumpers of a horse exiting away from me. All possible reasons for sub optimal performance and valuable knowledge to have going forward.

Chapter 20. Spurs

The use of spurs is where a bit of local awareness of the habits of both trainers and jockeys in one's racing area can be helpful. In my racing jurisdiction they are not notifiable as a gear change and hence only observable by being on track or via the vision feed.

Experience tells me that some riders use them as often as possible, others rarely and some seem to apply them as a strategic measure on horses that tend to be very laconic on race days, or those that are often tardy from the gates. Whatever the reason, previous knowledge of their use or not on a particular horse and a subsequent application change, can signal possible different tactical intent from the rider and trainer.

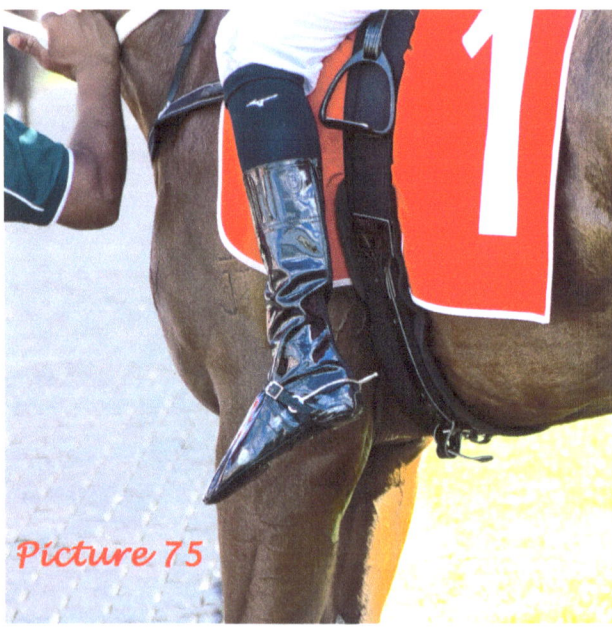

Picture 75

There is definitely a horse suitability factor at play here and most trainers would have their preferences as to when and to what type of horse they are applied. Their use is a lot less noticeable on young horses, first starters, fillies and excitable types. More prevalent on older geldings and horses that have plenty of racing experience.

As a paddock analyst, it is important to keep an eye out for any reaction from the horse when the spurs are used. I am always very vigilant when the horse and rider enter onto the track and the horse is given a little dig or tap with the spurs to trot or canter off and to note what the reaction was. This is more important if one's local knowledge, from previous observations, tells you that the horse is a first timer with spurs. A sudden spurt forward, toss of the head and then a struggle with the reins by the rider trying to settle the horse down is not the optimum mindset you want the horse going to the gates with. From a future point of view, if the horse was subjected to first time spurs use, had an adverse reaction at the canter off and subsequently raced ungenerously, it is good information going forward. It may have been the cause of a poor performance and removal of the spurs at the next race may be pertinent and an insight that few others would have.

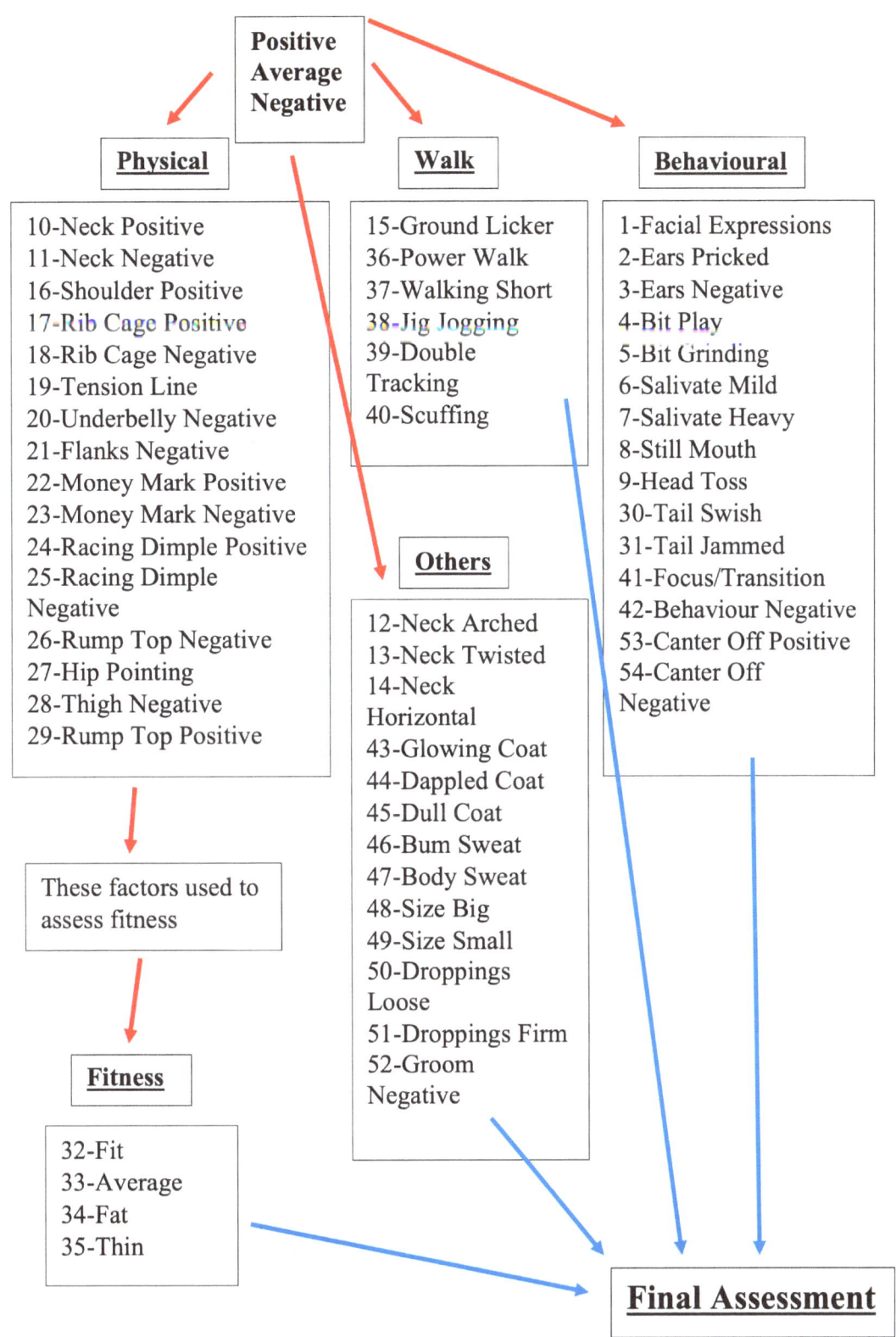

Chapter 21. Factor Discussion, Tables and Combinations

Factor Groupings

54 factors and 5 sundry items have been described in the previous chapters. The physical development of the musculature from head to tail, 4 overall fitness categories, 6 different walk patterns, 14 behavioural variables, 13 other factors comprised from health, external and environmental causes. Plus, bandages, spurs and other items to take note of, in the stalls, behind the gates and post-race. At this point it's hoped that the reader has reached a stage where they feel they understand the descriptions and are confident they can go on track or watch the TV stream and begin their journey of identifying the factors. Like learning most things, it's about practicing and watching. Try to be very observant. It's not difficult and most of the people I've introduced to it catch on very quickly.

Chart 1 gives an insight of the various assessment groups that the variables fall into. The first box in the chart, "Positive, Average, Negative", refers to the spectrum that has been used for the factor descriptions. Predominantly the pictures used have depicted the positive and negative extremes of the relevant variable. This was for descriptive purposes to try and clearly show the factor. It doesn't mean that the factors should be classed as present if they are only observed at the positive and negative extremes. Obviously, there are "degrees" of a variable's progression, especially in determining the fitness factors, and with experience through practice, the analyst can develop their own parameters for determining the "degrees" of when a factor is present, positive or negative. This in turn leads to consistency in variable categorisation. Everyone will develop and establish their own set of boundaries for classification. In a borderline fitness scenario, one analyst may go with Fit, while a second may go with Average. That's fine if they are consistent and adhere to the classification parameters, they have established for themselves.

The "Physical Structures" box consists of the ingredients used for slotting a horse into the Fit, Average, Fat and Thin gradings of the "Fitness Categories" box. This is the most common process the analyst will do at the yard. It's the first thing we would all want to know. Is this horse fit? All the physical structures that we assess are done visually. We can see the muscles and determine their stage of development and make a call. To determine how the horse may be feeling inside those muscles, the "Walks" box can be of assistance. The different categories can give us a guide to whether the horse is relaxed and loose, suggesting an absence of soreness, or jig jogging or walking short, suggesting some soreness or muscular niggle.

The "Behavioural" group of factors allows the analyst to reach an appraisal of the horse's state of mind. The "Others" group is comprised of some idiosyncratic factors, such as the neck carriages, to general health predictors like the coat conditions, to externally caused factors being the groom negativity or environmental conditions that can cause the sweat observations.

As the last box shows, all these groupings come together to let one form an opinion or "Final Assessment" of the horse pre-race. The novice horse watcher shouldn't be overwhelmed by thinking how they are going to manage assessing a full field of horses using 54 factors. It only takes a few meetings to get a handle on doing it and armed with the knowledge of what to look for, most walk away from their first meeting confident it's not a difficult or daunting task. Conversations often end with comments about all the horses they've bet on, that they shouldn't have, knowing what they now know.

In Table 1 – Factor Impact Values is a list of all the factors in their allotted Variable Number order, from 1 – 54 and the table has the count or number of observations, the Impact Value and the Rank of the IV. The counts are a reasonable representation of how often the factors occur, however, they were accumulated over two periods due to the covid interruption and some factors weren't collected in both periods, so some may occur marginally more, but it would be minimal.

Chapter 21. Factor Discussion, Tables and Combinations

As previously mentioned, one thing to remember is the decisions behind Impact Values are from my selections and observations at the mounting yard. I'm positive that those that get a grip on identifying the variables would return the same or similar IV's as myself. I've found the decisions of people I've associated with, or helped, very quickly begin to merge with my decisions to the point where we are seeing and identifying the same things regularly.

Impact Value strength can increase when you find an imbalance in a race. What this means is that the IV is relative to what factors are assigned to the opposition. Encountering this scenario is when "the horse watching edge" smacks you straight in the face.

Using Power Walk (51) as an example, with its IV of 1.87. If you clearly identify a power walker and the rest of the field is comprised of short walkers, sweaters, poor behaviour or just a field where no other strong positives exist, then the Power Walk IV is probably greater than the 1.87, which is an overall figure from 5422 observations and thousands of races. A form analysis analogy would be where a three-time distance winner is up against a field of competitors who have failed at the distance or are first time at the distance. That would be considered an important form edge and it's the same with pre-race horse factors. An important edge.

Many times, I've walked away from the mounting yard thinking "this is a one-horse race". A single horse with strong variables against a balance of average to poorly marked horses. Many form analysts would have encountered the same situation, I'm sure. Like all perceived "good things' in racing, the results don't always eventuate how we expect, but over time there is definitely an advantage when this set of horse factors is encountered.

The message here is that IV metrics can be dynamic, strengthening when the right scenario occurs and on the flip side, weakening when the opposition is strong, with many well marked contenders. Like most data points used in the analysis of trying to pick a winner they can have a "race specific" value.

Table 1 - Overall Factor Impact Values

Variable	Factor	Count	IV	Rank	Category
1	Facial Expressions	286	0.74	39	Behaviour
2	Ears Pricked	930	1.38	15	Behaviour
3	Ears Negative	562	0.6	47	Behaviour
4	Bit Play	4511	1.06	23	Behaviour
5	Bit Grinding	160	0.83	33	Behaviour
6	Salivate Mild	816	1.13	21	Body Function
7	Salivate Heavy	80	1.02	25	Body Function
8	Still Mouth	972	1.96	5	Behaviour
9	Head Toss	1306	0.78	36	Behaviour
10	Neck Positive	1275	1.93	6	Physicality
11	Neck Negative	267	0.61	46	Physicality
12	Neck Arched	743	1.38	15	Neck Carriage
13	Neck Twisted	622	1.5	13	Neck Carriage
14	Neck Horizontal	508	1.14	19	Neck Carriage
15	Ground Licker	505	1.71	9	Neck Carriage
16	Shoulder Positive	2571	1.3	18	Physicality
17	Rib Cage Positive	2767	1.8	8	Physicality

Chapter 21. Factor Discussion, Tables and Combinations

Variable	Factor	Count	IV	Rank	Category
18	Rib Cage Negative	8941	0.83	33	Physicality
19	Tension Line	1386	0.74	39	Physicality
20	Underbelly Negative	4980	0.45	51	Physicality
21	Flanks Negative	2188	0.68	43	Physicality
22	Money Mark Positive	3869	1.52	12	Physicality
23	Money Mark Negative	5232	0.74	39	Physicality
24	Racing Dimple Positive	9425	1.64	11	Physicality
25	Racing Dimple Negative	637	0.74	39	Physicality
26	Rump Top Negative	1090	0.56	49	Physicality
27	Hip Pointing	4450	0.68	43	Physicality
28	Thigh Negative	3304	0.6	47	Physicality
29	Rump Top Positive	1547	2.31	2	Physicality
30	Tail Swishing	1787	0.98	26	Behaviour
31	Tail Jammed	297	0.82	35	Behaviour
32	Fit	8689	2.09	4	Physicality
33	Average	14993	0.91	27	Physicality
34	Fat	5612	0.34	53	Physicality
35	Thin	2685	0.45	51	Physicality
36	Power Walk	5422	1.87	7	Walk
37	Walking Short	4592	0.86	31	Walk
38	Jig Jogging	4390	0.87	30	Walk
39	Double Tracking	578	1.05	24	Walk
40	Scuffing	91	0.22	54	Walk
41	Focus/Transition	592	3.06	1	Behaviour
42	Behaviour Negative	1403	0.76	38	Behaviour
43	Glowing Coat	768	1.46	14	Health
44	Dappled Coat	501	1.32	17	Health
45	Dull Coat	478	0.68	43	Health
46	Bum Sweat	1189	1.14	19	Body Function
47	Body Sweat	2502	0.85	32	Body Function
48	Size Big	666	1.13	21	Physicality
49	Size Small	207	0.88	28	Physicality
50	Droppings Loose	413	1.7	10	Body Function
51	Droppings Firm	738	0.88	28	Body Function
52	Groom Negative	164	0.78	36	Human
53	Canter Off Positive	682	2.1	3	Behaviour
54	Canter Off Negative	741	0.49	50	Behaviour

An interesting topic is where this standout situation is more likely to occur. In Australia our basic race meeting structure is metropolitan, provincial and country and the class and strength of the racing generally decreases in that order, as the prizemoney also does. As the fields slide down this scale and the class and prizemoney decreases, horse factor "separation" increases. By "separation" I mean the quality difference of the Impact Values across the field. There can be a broadening of the value range, tending to bias and group more toward the lower values due to the lower class of animal. This is where a standout is more likely to occur.

A metropolitan field will often have multiple well marked horses, provincial fields often the same or slightly less, with the country fields having even less quality and hence, if a competitor is observed with a strong variable, it's more likely to stand out against the opposition. These are broad descriptions of our racing class structure, but I've always found it's more common to find "separation" down the lower end of the scale.

From my experience overseas this would seem to hold true too. From the high quality of the Japan Racing Association tracks of Fuchu and Kyoto down to the Local Government courses such as Funabashi and Tokyo City Keiba. (Oi Racecourse). Similarly in America going from Belmont in New York City to Parx in Pennsylvania. The implication of all this is that not only is there value in being able to identify fitness and behavioural variables and make an assessment on a particular horse, but there is increased value in being able to recognise and evaluate if the strengths and weaknesses of the opposition, put you in a more favourable wagering position or not.

The IVs in Table 1, the other metrics used throughout the book, or whatever method you use to record your assessments, be that in your head, or scribbled on a form guide, and for those fortunate enough to have access, the advent of the Betfair Exchange provides the pre-race analyst with another opportunity. The ability to "Lay". This means the variables with poor IV's become just as important as those at the upper end. The horse watcher's knowledge can be used to pick a loser or a winner. Even though the exchange has been around for many years now, a lot of users including myself, have an imbedded mindset where we instinctively evaluate things on the back side, resulting in missed opportunities on the lay side.

An elderly gentleman who was a regular racegoer at the tracks I attended over the years, told me that for most of his punting life, breaking even was a good year, until he embraced laying horses on the exchange. Most of his success came from dismissing horses as chances based on his opinion of their behaviour and fitness in the parade ring. He was always at pains to tell me he was a very small bettor, but I could tell how pleased he was with his newfound betting success. Kudos to him for embracing new options and it has always served as a reminder to me of the opportunities and advantages, at both ends of the horse variable assessment scale.

Distance Effects

Table 2 looks at the effects of race distance on the Impact Values, with the distances broken up into the following groups to approximate the appropriate preferences for the sprinting, middle distance and staying horses.

      Short - <= 1235 metres or <= 6.17 furlongs
      Mid - 1300 metres to 1850 metres or 6.5 to 9.25 furlongs
      Long - > 1850 metres or > 9.25 furlongs

The obvious thing that should be expected, without looking at the table, is the difference in body shapes, from the sprinter to the stayer. A common analogy, that most should easily identify, is the comparison to human athletes. From the muscular, robust bodies of an Olympic track and field sprinter to the lean, wiry look of the longer distance runners. For the most part, equine frames follow the same range.

Table 2 - Factor Impact Values by Distance

Variable	Factor	Short	Mid	Long	Category
1	Facial Expressions	0.89	0.72	0.58	Behaviour
2	Ears Pricked	1.29	1.55	1.15	Behaviour

Chapter 21. Factor Discussion, Tables and Combinations

Variable	Factor	Short	Mid	Long	Category
3	Ears Negative	0.88	0.33	0.47	Behaviour
4	Bit Play	1.1	0.97	1.19	Behaviour
5	Bit Grinding	-	-	-	Behaviour
6	Salivate Mild	1.24	1.12	0.81	Body Function
7	Salivate Heavy	-	-	-	Body Function
8	Still Mouth	1.31	1.78	2.6	Behaviour
9	Head Toss	0.88	0.74	0.63	Behaviour
10	Neck Positive	2.09	1.72	2.02	Physicality
11	Neck Negative	0.11	0.76	0.52	Physicality
12	Neck Arched	1.5	1.24	1.42	Neck Carriage
13	Neck Twisted	1.63	1.27	1.64	Neck Carriage
14	Neck Horizontal	1.04	1.11	1.31	Neck Carriage
15	Ground Licker	1.42	1.86	1.89	Neck Carriage
16	Shoulder Positive	1.22	1.79	1.87	Physicality
17	Rib Cage Positive	1.76	1.77	1.92	Physicality
18	Rib Cage Negative	0.71	0.8	0.62	Physicality
19	Tension Line	0.74	0.76	0.74	Physicality
20	Underbelly Negative	0.49	0.37	0.52	Physicality
21	Flanks Negative	0.54	0.68	0.87	Physicality
22	Money Mark Positive	1.38	1.61	1.62	Physicality
23	Money Mark Negative	0.71	0.78	0.71	Physicality
24	Racing Dimple Positive	1.38	1.44	1.4	Physicality
25	Racing Dimple Negative	0.85	0.62	0.78	Physicality
26	Rump Top Negative	0.43	0.52	0.7	Physicality
27	Hip Pointing	0.58	0.67	0.78	Physicality
28	Thigh Negative	0.34	0.72	0.69	Physicality
29	Rump Top Positive	2.36	2.22	2.48	Physicality
30	Tail Swishing	1.03	0.94	0.95	Behaviour
31	Tail Jammed	1.28	0.74	0.16	Behaviour
32	Fit	2.05	2.08	2.13	Physicality
33	Average	0.89	0.92	0.92	Physicality
34	Fat	0.4	0.3	0.31	Physicality
35	Thin	0.33	0.5	0.46	Physicality
36	Power Walk	1.85	1.88	1.85	Walk
37	Walking Short	0.91	0.84	0.78	Walk
38	Jig Jogging	0.9	0.85	0.79	Walk
39	Double Tracking	1.1	1.06	0.93	Walk
40	Scuffing	-	-	-	Walk

Chapter 21. Factor Discussion, Tables and Combinations

Variable	Factor	Short	Mid	Long	Category
41	Focus/Transition	3.31	2.81	3.1	Behaviour
42	Behaviour Negative	0.82	0.74	0.69	Behaviour
43	Glowing Coat	1.66	1.29	1.25	Health
44	Dappled Coat	1.22	1.43	1.2	Health
45	Dull Coat	0.79	0.79	0.63	Health
46	Bum Sweat	1.3	1.05	1.02	Body Function
47	Body Sweat	0.77	0.96	0.85	Body Function
48	Size Big	1.27	1.03	1.43	Physicality
49	Size Small	0.41	1.18	1.42	Physicality
50	Droppings Loose	1.74	1.61	1.41	Body Function
51	Droppings Firm	0.85	0.87	0.9	Body Function
52	Groom Negative	-	-	-	Human
53	Canter Off Positive	1.91	2.01	2.36	Behaviour
54	Canter Off Negative	0.75	0.51	0.29	Behaviour

Table 2 really makes one aware, that race distance should be forefront in the parade ring analyst's mind when assessing a field. A strong example of this is two factors that pertain to the mouth of the horse, Variable 6 – Salivate Mild and Variable 8 – Still Mouth. Looking at the progression of the Impact Values for Salivate Mild from Short to Mid to Long, the returns are 1.24 to 1.12 to 0.81. A substantial decrease in IV as the race distance increases. Then for the Still Mouth factor there is a doubling of the IV's importance as distance increases. With Short at 1.31, Mid at 1.78 and Long at a 2.6 Impact Value.

Remembering that an IV of 1 means that the factor is winning at a rate that is considered normal for the population, Salivate Mild is 24% higher at 1.24 in the Sprinter but ends up a negative at 19% below what is average, for the stayer, at 0.81%. On the other hand, Still Mouth starts at a strong positive of 31% above normal for the short course horse and ends up at 160% above for the long-distance horses. It goes to show what an important factor to look for and identify Still Mouth is.

If we step back and try to evaluate why these two variables head in opposite directions, as the distance of the race increases, my explanation is that it comes down to the critical requirement that long distance horses need to breathe properly in a race. How often do we hear a winning jockey say the horse travelled well and was in a very good breathing pattern? Or the trainer's instructions for the rider are to take a position in the field where the horse is comfortable and breathing rhythmically. Referencing back to the descriptions of the two factors, it's understandable how the Impact Values take the directions they do. The longer a horse runs, the more likely it's respiratory system will be affected. So, with a Still Mouth you are starting from a point, in the parade ring, where the horse is completely unaffected by any issues of the mouth, and hence, more likely to maintain that in the race. Whereas, with the Salivate Mild horse, there has been some activity in the mouth to cause the saliva production. The Impact Value tells us that the short course horse can get by with it, but clearly not the long-distance horse.

In the next two tables (3,4), we look at the Impact Values in the Short and Long categories and group them by the movement of those values. Those that became more positive or maintained their positivity and those that increased in negativity as distance increased.

Table 3 - Factors with Increased or Maintained Positivity-Short to Long Distance

Variable	Factor	Short IV	Long IV	Category
2	Ears Pricked	1.29	1.15	Behaviour

Chapter 21. Factor Discussion, Tables and Combinations

Variable	Factor	Short IV	Long IV	Category
4	Bit Play	1.1	1.19	Behaviour
8	Still Mouth	1.31	2.6	Behaviour
10	Neck Positive	2.09	2.02	Physicality
12	Neck Arched	1.5	1.42	Neck Carriage
13	Neck Twisted	1.63	1.64	Neck Carriage
14	Neck Horizontal	1.04	1.31	Neck Carriage
15	Ground Licker	1.42	1.89	Neck Carriage
16	Shoulder Positive	1.22	1.87	Physicality
17	Rib Cage Positive	1.76	1.92	Physicality
22	Money Mark Positive	1.38	1.62	Physicality
24	Racing Dimple Positive	1.38	1.4	Physicality
29	Rump Top Positive	2.36	2.48	Physicality
32	Fit	2.05	2.13	Physicality
36	Power Walk	1.85	1.85	Walks
41	Focus/Transition	3.31	3.1	Behaviour
43	Glowing Coat	1.66	1.25	Health
44	Dappled Coat	1.22	1.2	Health
46	Bum Sweat	1.3	1.02	Behaviour
48	Size Big	1.27	1.43	Physicality
50	Droppings Loose	1.74	1.41	Health
53	Canter Off Positive	1.91	2.36	Behaviour

Table 4 – Factors that Increase in Negativity – Short to Long Distance

Variable	Factor	Short IV	Long IV	Category
1	Facial Expressions	0.89	0.58	Behaviour
3	Ears Negative	0.88	0.47	Behaviour
9	Head Toss	0.88	0.63	Behaviour
18	Rib Cage Negative	0.71	0.62	Physicality
25	Racing Dimple Negative	0.85	0.78	Physicality
34	Fat	0.4	0.31	Physicality
37	Walking Short	0.91	0.78	Walks
42	Behaviour Negative	0.82	0.69	Behaviour
45	Dull Coat	0.79	0.63	Health
54	Canter Off Negative	0.75	0.29	Behaviour

Something to note is that of all the 54 factors, only 3 variables change their positive or negative IV status from the Overall value in Table 1 to the different distance values in Table 2. They are, Salivate Mild as discussed previously, Tail Jammed and Size Small. What will change over distance is the relevance, importance, or the Impact Value of the variables. Negatives will remain negatives and positives will stay positive, but their IV's will change importance, accordingly. Table 3 illustrates this, showing some large increases in IVs as races get longer. Table 4 depicts the deterioration in Impact Values of factors due to increased race distance. So, Table 3 shows us things we should like to see in stayers and Table 4 factors that we wouldn't like to see.

There are negative factors that actually increase in IV from a sprinter to a stayer. They are still negative but of less severity. They are Flanks Negative, Rump Top Negative, Hip Pointing, Thigh Negative and the overall fitness category, Thin. Interestingly, they are all factors of the rear end and the reason for that, is somewhat understandable. It likely occurs due to the body shape of stayers, as was previously discussed. Being a relatively leaner and lighter appearing body style of horse, it may come down to decisions made in marking them as negative variables. Possibly a combination of marking error and the greater prevalence of horses with borderline factors being able to win, down at this staying end of the scale.

Table 3 also exemplifies the importance of the neck carriage, especially in the staying horse. It is definitely a sign of a relaxed horse and virtually an essential requirement for a horse racing over distance. Low neck carriages are also indicative of class, in a sprinting horse. For years I've heard people at the parade ring comment on a horse they believe is "raring to go". It's usually up on its toes, jig jogging, with its head held up high due to an elevated neck. The data would say this is a fallacy and I've always believed that to be so too. It's the opposite that one should prefer to see. Some of the world's best sprinters gathered in Hong Kong recently for an international sprint race and nearly the whole field paraded with a nice loose walk and horizontal, or lower, neck carriages. The same occurred here in Australia for a Group One 1000 metre sprint, that included the highest rated sprinter in the world, Nature Strip. The entire field had low neck carriages, with two having Twisted Neck and all had flowing, lengthy walks. The best attributes of the stayer are also the best attributes of the sprinter.

Breaking down the Overall Impact Values of Table 1, into the distance categories of Table 2, has provided knowledge for the yard analyst to be further equipped to closely assess the value of what one is witnessing in the parade ring. In addition to that, Table 5 examines the effects of market efficiency on the Overall Impact Values of Table 1. How do the odds affect the importance of the variables we are identifying in the parade paddock? Is the IV of a $2.50 Rump Top Positive horse the same as a $20 Rump Top Positive rival?

Market Influences

The prices used in Table 5 are Betfair Exchange prices, taken around three minutes before the off. They are not Betfair SP prices, they are real time odds. The factor values for Salivate Heavy (7), Scuffing (40) and Groom Negative (52) weren't calculated, as the number of observations thinned out too much for a reliable analysis to be achieved. The Difference columns, for both the <$6 bracket and the <$11group, relate to the Overall IV figures and not to each other.

The Impact Values of the <$11 group tend to show more variation in their movements than the <$6 bracket, but at the firmer prices of the <$6 group, any factor that had an Overall IV above the benchmark figure of one remained above it. There was movement both ways, up and down, but they all stayed positive. The main market influence on the factors in the <$6 group, that had Overall IV's below one, was that they all increased their IV's bar one, Rib Cage Negative (18), which went from 0.83 to 0.61. Only three variables turned from below one to above one. Head Toss (9) went from 0.78 to 1.04, Tail Jammed (31) from 0.82 to 1.08 and Droppings Firm (51) from 0.88 to 1.01.Tail Swishing (30) went from 0.98 to 1.01 which is around the average of one anyway and I wouldn't consider it a significant enough move to be included.

Table 5 – Market Influence on Impact Values

Variable	Factor	Overall IV	<$6 IV	Difference	<$11 IV	Difference
1	Facial Expressions	0.74	0.92	0.18	0.92	0.18
2	Ears Pricked	1.38	1.1	-0.28	1.04	-0.34
3	Ears Negative	0.6	0.86	0.26	0.9	0.30
4	Bit Play	1.06	1.03	-0.03	0.84	-0.22

Chapter 21. Factor Discussion, Tables and Combinations

Variable	Factor	Overall IV	<$6 IV	Difference	<$11 IV	Difference
5	Bit Grinding	0.83	0.94	0.11	0.81	-0.02
6	Salivate Mild	1.13	1.07	-0.06	1.08	-0.05
7	Salivate Heavy	1.02	0	0.00	0	0.00
8	Still Mouth	1.96	2.02	0.06	1.71	-0.25
9	Head Toss	0.78	1.04	0.26	0.93	0.15
10	Neck Positive	1.93	1.98	0.05	1.36	-0.57
11	Neck Negative	0.61	0.73	0.12	0.91	0.30
12	Neck Arched	1.38	1.13	-0.25	1.12	-0.26
13	Neck Twisted	1.5	1.19	-0.31	1.23	-0.27
14	Neck Horizontal	1.14	1.07	-0.07	1.02	-0.12
15	Ground Licker	1.71	1.81	0.10	1.08	-0.63
16	Shoulder Positive	1.3	1.41	0.11	1.27	-0.03
17	Rib Cage Positive	1.8	1.65	-0.15	1.23	-0.57
18	Rib Cage Negative	0.83	0.61	-0.22	0.83	0.00
19	Tension Line	0.74	0.88	0.14	0.92	0.18
20	Underbelly Negative	0.45	0.78	0.33	0.74	0.29
21	Flanks Negative	0.68	0.75	0.07	0.78	0.10
22	Money Mark Positive	1.52	1.76	0.24	1.25	-0.27
23	Money Mark Negative	0.74	0.89	0.15	0.84	0.10
24	Racing Dimple Positive	1.64	1.54	-0.10	1.13	-0.51
25	Racing Dimple Negative	0.74	0.89	0.15	0.89	0.15
26	Rump Top Negative	0.56	0.83	0.27	0.78	0.22
27	Hip Pointing	0.68	0.77	0.09	0.89	0.21
28	Thigh Negative	0.6	0.88	0.28	0.75	0.15
29	Rump Top Positive	2.31	2.39	0.08	1.52	-0.79
30	Tail Swishing	0.98	1.01	0.03	0.98	0.00
31	Tail Jammed	0.82	1.08	0.26	0.98	0.16
32	Fit	2.09	2.18	0.09	1.31	-0.78
33	Average	0.91	0.91	0.00	0.89	-0.02
34	Fat	0.34	0.77	0.43	0.61	0.27
35	Thin	0.45	0.79	0.34	0.73	0.28
36	Power Walk	1.87	1.9	0.03	1.22	-0.65
37	Walking Short	0.86	0.93	0.07	0.93	0.07
38	Jig Jogging	0.87	0.97	0.10	0.95	0.08
39	Double Tracking	1.05	1.05	0.00	1.16	0.11
40	Scuffing	0.22	0	0	0	0
41	Focus/Transition	3.06	2.88	-0.18	1.9	-1.16
42	Behaviour Negative	0.76	0.79	0.03	0.97	0.21
43	Glowing Coat	1.46	1.62	0.16	1.11	-0.35
44	Dappled Coat	1.32	1.38	0.06	1.12	-0.20

Chapter 21. Factor Discussion, Tables and Combinations

Variable	Factor	Overall IV	<$6 IV	Difference	<$11 IV	Difference
45	Dull Coat	0.68	0.9	0.22	0.88	0.20
46	Bum Sweat	1.14	1.25	0.11	1.04	-0.10
47	Body Sweat	0.85	0.91	0.06	0.92	0.07
48	Size Big	1.13	1.3	0.17	1.03	-0.10
49	Size Small	0.88	0.95	0.07	0.82	-0.06
50	Droppings Loose	1.7	1.86	0.16	1.22	-0.48
51	Droppings Firm	0.88	1.01	0.13	0.94	0.06
52	Groom Negative	0.78	0	0	0	0
53	Canter Off Positive	2.1	2.41	0.31	1.48	-0.62
54	Canter Off Negative	0.49	0.68	0.19	0.62	0.13

Two other variables in the <$6 group came close to normal, Jig Jogging (38) and Size Small (49). Using Jig Jogging as an example, if say the situation arose where a wagering decision had to be made on a $3 jig jogger and we know now that the IV at that price is practically normal, or average at 0.97, my advice is that the decision is dependent on what other factors are present, especially the fitness categories. As will be shown in the combination tables, the strong IV of a Fit (32) graded horse has the ability to keep the $3 Fit/Jig Jogger combination very positive.

The general influence of the efficiency of the betting market on factor values, particularly in the <$6 bracket, is that it raises the IV of the negative values, maintains values of positive factors and in a lot of instances, increases positivity. Market efficiency commands market respect and in turn, this should be applied to horse watching factors, just as price influences form factors. Table 5 provides an insight into the value changes that odds can cause and lets you know where you stand when making decisions, the same as the distance influences previously looked at do and just as the Combinations, we will now look at do.

Combinations

In Tables 6,7,8 and 9 we look at what effect the combining of factors has, both positive and negative, on the Impact Values of the four fitness categories. Fit (32), Average (33), Fat (34) and Thin (35). The physical factors that we use to comprise the fitness categories are excluded, as that would be doubling up on their values. The top half of the tables, down to where variable number 53 is combined with the relevant fitness variable, 32,33,34, or 35, are those that have a positive Overall IV from Table 1 and the lower half are the negatives. Column 4 is the difference between the relevant fitness categories Overall IV, from Table 1 and the Combination IV in Column 3. In the heading of Column 4 in the Fit table, the Overall IV for Fit is shown, 2.09 and so the values in that column are the variations in IVs from the 2.09 and the Combination IVs. This is where we see the effect the added factors have on the fitness Impact Values.

The tables show two factor combinations, as the observation numbers tend to thin out as more variables are added, however, on the analysis I did on larger combinations with reliable enough observation counts, the trends seen in the two factor combinations were the same. Further positive factors meant increased or maintained positivity and additional negative factors decreased the values.

Table 6 – Fit (32) Combinations

Variables	Combination	Combination IV's	Diff from Fit 2.09
32/2	Fit, Ears Pricked	2.78	0.69
32/4	Fit, Bit Play	2.32	0.23

Chapter 21. Factor Discussion, Tables and Combinations

Variables	Combination	Combination IV's	Diff from Fit 2.09
32/6	Fit, Mild Salivation	2.19	0.10
32/8	Fit, Still Mouth	2.26	0.17
32/12	Fit, Neck Arched	2.8	0.71
32/13	Fit, Neck Twisted	2.73	0.64
32/14	Fit, Neck Horizontal	2.05	-0.04
32/15	Fit, Ground Licker	2.51	0.42
32/36	Fit, Power Walk	3.19	1.10
32/39	Fit, Double Tracking	2.16	0.07
32/41	Fit, Focus/Transition	3.7	1.61
32/43	Fit, Glowing Coat	1.88	-0.21
32/44	Fit, Dappled Coat	2	-0.09
32/46	Fit, Bum Sweat	1.98	-0.11
32/48	Fit, Size Big	1.55	-0.54
32/50	Fit, Droppings Loose	2.33	0.24
32/53	Fit, Canter Off Positive	2.58	0.49
32/1	Fit, Facial Expressions	1.88	-0.21
32/3	Fit, Ears Negative	1.71	-0.38
32/5	Fit, Bit Grinding	1.84	-0.25
32/9	Fit, Head Toss	1.58	-0.51
32/19	Fit, Tension Line	1.94	-0.15
32/30	Fit, Tail Swishing	1.69	-0.40
32/31	Fit, Tail Jammed	1.68	-0.41
32/37	Fit, Walking Short	1.97	-0.12
32/38	Fit, Jig Jogging	1.98	-0.11
32/42	Fit, Behaviour Negative	1.52	-0.57
32/45	Fit, Dull Coat	1.81	-0.28
32/47	Fit, Body Sweat	1.86	-0.23
32/49	Fit, Size Small	1.69	-0.40
32/51	Fit, Droppings Firm	2.06	-0.03
32/52	Fit, Groom Negative	2.01	-0.08
32/54	Fit, Canter Off Negative	1.23	-0.86

Table 6 shows that most of the positive variables added to "Fit" returned increased or similar Impact Values, except for Size Big, -0.54 and Glowing Coat -0.21. The two strongest positive additions were, Focus/Transition, at a +1.61 increase and Power Walk, at +1.1 increase. These two factors, combined with Fit, actually come close to a description of the "perfect" pre-race presentation of a racehorse. A fit, low neck, loose walking, well behaved, focused competitor.

Looking at the negative combinations, the three biggest decreases were with Head Toss, at -0.51, Behaviour Negative at -0.57 and Canter Off Negative at -0.86. Interestingly, they are all from the general Behaviour group. All negative additions caused a reduction in the Impact Value of Fit, but the strong IV of the Fit horse, displays its ability to absorb some negative factors, with all the values remaining very high. The general trend appears to be that additional positive factors equates to increased IVs and a slight reduction

Chapter 21. Factor Discussion, Tables and Combinations

occurs with a negative addition. Multiple negatives would cause an exponential deterioration of the Impact Value.

Table 6 is a good illustration of the strength and resilience of the Fit variable and amplifies the importance of the horse watchers' requirement of being able and competent, at identifying all the physical attributes, that comprise the Fit category.

In Table 7, the Average fitness category combinations, there is a minimal decrease in the Bit Play factor of -0.04, but the remainder of the positive additions to Average all increased or maintained their Impact Values. Several of the combinations pushed well into strong IV ranges, assisted by some of the higher rated variables from the Overall IVs of Table 1. With Neck Twisted, Ground Licker, Power Walk, Focus/Transition, Droppings Loose and Canter Off Positive all joining in to exert their influence. So, the data here would imply that if the situation occurs where the analyst has had to make a decision on a borderline Fit or Average judgement, the presence of one of the power variables in the horse would ensure the Impact Value is elevated well above the one mark.

Table 7 – Average (33) Combinations

Variables	Combination	Combination IV's	Diff from Average 0.91
33/2	Average, Ears Pricked	0.99	0.08
33/4	Average, Bit Play	0.87	-0.04
33/6	Average, Mild Salivation	0.98	0.07
33/8	Average, Still Mouth	1.11	0.20
33/12	Average, Neck Arched	1.02	0.11
33/13	Average, Neck Twisted	1.3	0.39
33/14	Average, Neck Horizontal	0.94	0.03
33/15	Average, Ground Licker	1.41	0.50
33/36	Average, Power Walk	1.4	0.49
33/39	Average, Double Tracking	0.91	0.00
33/41	Average, Focus/Transition	2.54	1.63
33/43	Average, Glowing Coat	1.17	0.26
33/44	Average, Dappled Coat	1.17	0.26
33/46	Average, Bum Sweat	1.05	0.14
33/48	Average, Size Big	0.97	0.06
33/50	Average, Droppings Loose	1.48	0.57
33/53	Average, Canter Off Positive	1.86	0.95
33/1	Average, Facial Expressions	0.59	-0.32
33/3	Average, Ears Negative	0.65	-0.26
33/5	Average, Bit Grinding	0.64	-0.27
33/9	Average, Head Toss	0.85	-0.06
33/19	Average, Tension Line	0.68	-0.23
33/30	Average, Tail Swishing	0.98	0.07
33/31	Average, Tail Jammed	0.72	-0.19
33/37	Average, Walking Short	0.76	-0.15
33/38	Average, Jig Jogging	0.74	-0.17

Chapter 21. Factor Discussion, Tables and Combinations

Variables	Combination	Combination IV's	Diff from Average 0.91
33/42	Average, Behaviour Negative	0.87	-0.04
33/45	Average, Dull Coat	0.59	-0.32
33/47	Average, Body Sweat	0.84	-0.07
33/49	Average, Size Small	0.52	-0.39
33/51	Average, Droppings Firm	0.74	-0.17
33/52	Average, Groom Negative	0.63	-0.28
33/54	Average, Canter Off Negative	0.41	-0.50

Down in the negative group, we start to see the decay in Impact Values, where questionable fitness levels are met with adverse variables. The combinations here expose the territory where uncertainty in a competitor's winning probabilities start to prevail. Looking ahead to the Fat and Thin tables confirms that the "Average plus negative" pairing, is the beginning of the decline in Impact Values and the pivot point for making betting decisions in win markets. It's completely understandable that the figures bear this out as we're dealing with a horse that's been graded at less than optimum fitness and on top of that, is presenting with a negative attribute as well.

Table 8 – Fat (34) Combinations

Variables	Combination	Combination IV's	Diff from Fat 0.34
34/2	Fat, Ears Pricked	0.59	0.25
34/4	Fat, Bit Play	0.46	0.12
34/6	Fat, Mild Salivation	0.43	0.09
34/8	Fat, Still Mouth	0.39	0.05
34/12	Fat, Neck Arched	0.68	0.34
34/13	Fat, Neck Twisted	0.73	0.39
34/14	Fat, Neck Horizontal	0.27	-0.07
34/15	Fat, Ground Licker	0.81	0.47
34/36	Fat, Power Walk	0.53	0.19
34/39	Fat, Double Tracking	0.72	0.38
34/41	Fat, Focus/Transition	0.68	0.34
34/43	Fat, Glowing Coat	0.81	0.47
34/44	Fat, Dappled Coat	0.38	0.04
34/46	Fat, Bum Sweat	0.16	-0.18
34/48	Fat, Size Big	0.3	-0.04
34/50	Fat, Droppings Loose	0.56	0.22
34/53	Fat, Canter Off Positive	0.62	0.28
34/1	Fat, Facial Expressions	0.36	0.02
34/3	Fat, Ears Negative	0.27	-0.07
34/5	Fat, Bit Grinding	0.15	-0.19
34/9	Fat, Head Toss	0.43	0.09
34/19	Fat, Tension Line	0.33	-0.01
34/30	Fat, Tail Swishing	0.29	-0.05

Chapter 21. Factor Discussion, Tables and Combinations

Variables	Combination	Combination IV's	Diff from Fat 0.34
34/31	Fat, Tail Jammed	0.34	0.00
34/37	Fat, Walking Short	0.42	0.08
34/38	Fat, Jig Jogging	0.39	0.05
34/42	Fat, Behaviour Negative	0.11	-0.23
34/45	Fat, Dull Coat	0.28	-0.06
34/47	Fat, Body Sweat	0.12	-0.22
34/49	Fat, Size Small	0.51	0.17
34/51	Fat, Droppings Firm	0.22	-0.12
34/52	Fat, Groom Negative	0.34	0.00
34/54	Fat, Canter Off Negative	0.27	-0.07

The Impact Value returns shown in Table 8 – "Fat Combinations", for both positive and negative additions, are self-explanatory and what one would expect. With a horse race being an athletic event it's no surprise to see that "Fat" horses, even when supported by some of the power variables, are basically removed as any sort of competitive chances. There will always be exceptions to the rule, but generally they are better dealt with on the "lay" side, if that is an option.

Once again, the IVs highlight the importance of knowing the variables that comprise a "Fat" assessment and having the ability to identify the fitness categorisations. Make no mistake, opportunities will arise to dismiss "Fat" graded horses as wagering propositions. Be they quality horses, in quality races, or strong in the market. Often occurs with well performed, class horses returning from a break, or those that may have missed some training due to a small injury or setback. Their trainers may be racing them into fitness, they aren't fully fit, don't fit into the "average" variable and are clearly in need of a conditioning race. Don't let their quality, class or market position put you off. If you believe they are "Fat", then accept the opportunity or edge.

In the Thin combinations of Table 9 the largest Impact Value increases are again due to the addition of the dominant variables. The Thin/Power Walk combination is even elevated to just over the benchmark IV figure of one. The value of the "Neck Carriage" is also displayed, as all variables in that category caused an increase. In the lower half of the table, there is nearly across the board deterioration of IVs when a negative is in partnership with the Thin graded horse.

Table 9 – Thin (35) Combinations

Variables	Combination	Combination IV's	Diff from Thin 0.45
35/2	Thin, Ears Pricked	0.46	0.01
35/4	Thin, Bit Play	0.16	-0.29
35/6	Thin, Mild Salivation	0.23	-0.22
35/8	Thin, Still Mouth	0.68	0.23
35/12	Thin, Neck Arched	0.51	0.06
35/13	Thin, Neck Twisted	0.84	0.39
35/14	Thin, Neck Horizontal	0.98	0.53
35/15	Thin, Ground Licker	0.72	0.27
35/36	Thin, Power Walk	1.02	0.57
35/39	Thin, Double Tracking	0.42	-0.03

Chapter 21. Factor Discussion, Tables and Combinations

Variables	Combination	Combination IV's	Diff from Thin 0.45
35/41	Thin, Focus/Transition	0.56	0.11
35/43	Thin, Glowing Coat	0.72	0.27
35/44	Thin, Dappled Coat	0.63	0.18
35/46	Thin, Bum Sweat	0.2	-0.25
35/48	Thin, Size Big	1.07	0.62
35/50	Thin, Droppings Loose	0.73	0.28
35/53	Thin, Canter Off Positive	0.81	0.36
35/1	Thin, Facial Expressions	0.41	-0.04
35/3	Thin, Ears Negative	0.13	-0.32
35/5	Thin, Bit Grinding	0.51	0.06
35/9	Thin, Head Toss	0.12	-0.33
35/19	Thin, Tension Line	0.16	-0.29
35/30	Thin, Tail Swishing	0.09	-0.36
35/31	Thin, Tail Jammed	0.36	-0.09
35/37	Thin, Walking Short	0.39	-0.06
35/38	Thin, Jig Jogging	0.39	-0.06
35/42	Thin, Behaviour Negative	0.42	-0.03
35/45	Thin, Dull Coat	0.33	-0.12
35/47	Thin, Body Sweat	0.06	-0.39
35/49	Thin, Size Small	0.28	-0.17
35/51	Thin, Droppings Firm	0.3	-0.15
35/52	Thin, Groom Negative	0.45	0.00
35/54	Thin, Canter Off Negative	0.31	-0.14

Observing Factor Changes

What's being referred to here is a change in identified variables, both positive and negative, from one run to the next. As an example, a horse may have been graded as "Average" fitness last start and at a subsequent run has now presented as "Fit". Similarly, a horse may have paraded without any behavioural issues, but now is violently head tossing.

A lot of emphasis is placed on these race-to-race improvements and regressions, and it may be rightly so, but my thought is that to use that factor change, in isolation, as a trigger for a bet, may not be the way to go. I've always taken the position that the factor profile allotted to the horse on the day, is more relevant to the race day opposition's profiles, than a race-to-race improvement step within that allotted profile. Just because a serious head tosser at its previous run presents at its current run with a horizontal neck carriage, it shouldn't constitute a wager on the horse for that improvement alone. Although it's a good thing for the horse's profile, I would prefer to assess all the competitors' improvements and regressions and be swayed by the final factor profile information. It's a sum tally situation and any race-to-race changes are factored into the current overall appraisal anyway.

A pitfall of the race-to-race factor change scenario that I seem to come across quite regularly is with the sweating variable. Many yard analysts will comment on how a horse was sweating profusely last outing, but is bone dry at its current outing. On face value that comment may make the horse an attractive proposition to some, but there is a relevance issue often at play here. As we are aware, environmental factors, like heat and humidity, affect the levels of sweat output. At a horse's previous race all horses may have been sweating in humid and hot conditions and therefore it was normal to do so, but now at the next race, prevailing conditions are very mild, and one wouldn't expect much sweating to occur. So, in this situation there really is no change from a profuse sweater to being bone dry. Both were normal for the day, but a lot of credit is often given for this perceived change.

Less commonly I've seen this scenario occur with strong winds and flies. Parading horses have become very stirred up in windy conditions and flies have caused a lot of tail swishing and irritation that have led to behavioural issues. All understandable reactions, but at their next start they've been praised for their improved demeanour. So, there is often a relevance factor involved in the assessment of race-to-race factor change and it is well worthwhile for a yard analyst to be aware of these situations and be able to recognise the change in its correct context. Or just ignore any changes and go by your appraisals in the prevailing conditions.

Factor Profiling

Using a horse's variable profile from past recorded data, one's notes or recollections, may be slightly contradictory to what I just advocated for in the change section, that is, going by what one sees on the day, however there is a case for knowing the variable range of a horse's winning or losing efforts. A lot of variation occurs across the racehorse population in their presentation of fitness and demeanour factors and the analyst can never be one hundred per cent accurate, so knowing a horse's profile can be insightful.

This is especially applicable to the punter that has found a horse they like through their form study, has knowledge of a previous parade and just wants to head to the parade ring and check if it's presenting within the parameters they've seen before. This punter isn't interested in assessing other runners, they are looking for final reassurance to proceed with their form-based wager. A sensible approach and the value of having some horse factor experience. Horses have various race condition preferences, such as going, distance etc., and can also have a fitness and behaviour range where they may perform best. When the stars align and optimum form factors meet with optimum fitness and behaviour profiles, then a strong combination is created, and it is worthwhile being in a position to be able to take advantage of the situation.

A common progression of how a horse reaches its best performance profile may begin with a horse returning from a break. The horse may display variables implying edginess, like jig jogging, bit play and head tossing, and these factors tend to dissipate at subsequent runs until the horse parades well behaved, with improved fitness and turns in a good or winning run. This pattern, is of course, dependant on how trainers like to prepare their runners. Some have them ready to go, whereas others may prefer to race them into fitness. It may also be down to the type of horse makeup too, with gross types needing runs to gain peak fitness.

This winning or losing profiling can even come down to one particular factor. I recall a quality, but very quirky, Godolphin stable horse, that would parade with all sorts of different variables each race. Nothing in its past mounting yard variables showed any sort of consistency that was useable as a positive performance profile, a complete tossed salad of variables, but once it moved out of the yard onto the track, it displayed a variable that could be relied on to predict its performance. How it was going to run could be defined by the "Canter Off" variable. Always a good or winning run when it was "Canter Off Positive" and the opposite when "Canter Off Negative". This was true for a hundred percent of the times I viewed it and even for two interstate runs that I watched on the TV. The reason this horse came on my radar was because the first time I assessed it, its canter off was the epitome of what you want to see in that factor, and it stuck in my mind. The second time I saw it, it was head tossing and very difficult to control and raced poorly, so from then on, I took an interest in it, and it ran true to the "Canter Off" factor every time. Would be nice if they were all like that.

This profiling supports a strong argument for keeping notes of what the yard watcher sees. There's a good deal of comfort knowing that the horse you may fancy from form study parades with a group of variables that you know has previously proved successful. Also comfort in avoiding a bad wager when the opposite parade occurs.

Age and Stage of Training Preparation

With 2-year-olds, first starters and young inexperienced horses, one of the main things to look for is professionalism. Do they act brand new with negative behavioural factors and excitability or are they taking things in their stride and parading like they have done it a thousand times before. The latter is the type more likely to perform well. Look for the pricked ears, low neck carriage, calm walk, good behavioural factors, an affable compliance with their grooms' commands and take a close look at what the head is doing. Is the horse looking at all the distractions and just sensibly absorbing it and moving on unphased? These are the professional types that are showing us they know their business and are ready to perform.

Young horses vary in their ability to adapt to racing and at early stages of their career they may well be the most talented and fastest in a race, but their results may be thwarted by their lack of experience and race acumen. So, in this scenario the business like, professional profile type may often have an advantage.

Another scenario worth monitoring is a horse going from its first racing preparation into its second preparation. Huge leaps in improved behavioural patterns are often observed at the parade ring. The previously nervy, apprehensive, jig jogging baby has shed all those negatives and returned as a well-behaved horse, aware of what confronts it, but unperturbed. This is a common progression in young horses.

A further situation to be aware of, that may benefit the horse watcher, is the stage of the horse's preparation it is currently at. They can generally or loosely fall into these categories – first up from a spell, second up, third or fourth run back and multiple runs for the preparation.

Firstly, with those beginning their racing program back from a spell, what the yard analyst will see is very much a mixed bag and usually determined by the trainer and what they've deemed suitable for the horse. Some may require racing to improve fitness and hence may fall into the lower fitness categories, whilst others may not quite be at peak fitness but are produced fresh and capable of a forward showing. Some may be presented at peak fitness, ready to go, even over a long distance. That situation is not as prevalent in Australia as in say, Europe, where horses race first up over distance. In Australia they tend to increase distance with each run. However they present and however the analyst assesses them, it can be helpful to know what stage of racing they are at and whether the yard assessment correlates to a previous yard assessment and performance, if known.

I've always been interested in grading horses that are having their second run back in their racing program, due to the so called "second up syndrome". This is where a horse produces a very good run when resuming and then returns a flat or poor performance at the second run. Expectations are for an improved showing from the promising first effort due to the extra fitness and training, but that doesn't occur. It doesn't happen in all horses all the time or repeat in affected horses each time in their first to second races.

Having paid a lot of attention to this over the years, both from kept data and the visual perspective from the yard, I reached the assumption that some horses may be in a transient phase between "fresh and fit" and hence the regression in performance.

A slashing first up run often coincided with variables indicative of a fresh horse. One that is not fully fit, but enough to be competitive, with some jig jogging, strong on the groom's lead, mild salivation and an eagerness to get out there and get on with it without being behaviourally out of control. The second race variables were descriptive of a somewhat more subdued horse. A normal, plain walk, average fitness but progressing and no negatives, just very much your average parader. These were the most common set of circumstances that were apparent with the "second up syndrome", but the whole situation was somewhat inconsistent and good luck trying to predict it. Along with my assumption that the horse is transitioning from fresh to fit, there's probably other factors involved on the form side such as days between runs, training techniques, track conditions and so on.

In Australia with our racing and training styles and methods we would generally expect to see horses at their third and fourth run present in the yard at their peak fitness and be usually racing at their preferred distance. The paddock watcher should be inspecting the horses closely for variables that comprise good fitness judgements. Positive muscle developments of the neck and shoulder, slight rib cage coverage, well defined muscle build in the rear end with a positive rump top and a smooth walk with a low neck carriage. Those at their third or fourth run in displaying poor walks, elevated necks, head tossing and negative behaviours etc may be telling us that they may have some issues through soreness, or coping with the training and racing regimen, when it's reasonable for us to expect that they should be at their optimum racing condition level.

Horses that have had multiple runs and are getting deep into long preparations should be monitored for signs of training off, having had enough. This can present both physically and via demeanours. Signals to look for among many, are negative walks, head tossing, negative ears, tension line, tail swishing, dull coat and sweating. All signs that the animal, attitude wise, possibly doesn't want to be there.

The first sign physically is usually the "turning point" factor- Hip Pointing. Protrusion of the hip precedes factors of the rear end indicative of training off such as muscle depletion across the rump top and down through the thighs, with the horse taking on an angular, flat muscled appearance behind the saddle.

Some horses can withstand many runs and long preparations and maintain good physical structure along with a positive attitude and having advanced skills to identify those that can't opens an advantage or edge over the bulk of other punters.

Trainer Styles

Regular horse watching enables familiarity with how stables present their horses. After a while, in some instances, one can almost pick which stable the horse is from as soon as it enters the parade ring. Not because of the bridle, gear or groom, but by the style of the horse and its muscle conditioning. Trainers tend to have their own preferred "end product", so to speak, in how they like to present them visually on race day. There are obviously other factors involved that create the situation of trainers being capable of having horses look very similar and there is a vast variation in those appearances across the training ranks. Not just from the upper echelon down to the smaller trainers, but appearance variation through the varying levels of trainers.

Here's how I would categorise some of the fitness styles that I've become familiar with-

*** Large well defined muscle bulk, forward of the saddle, with well-built rear ends and an obvious portrayal of quality.

*** The tighter, leaner look, with clear muscle definition, but with no hip protrusion or angular appearance. Some top trainers who favour this appearance, where they are rock hard fit and possibly on the edge of going over the top, are clearly expert at their craft. I've often looked at these types thinking this race will be its last before a break, but no, time and time again they present in the same fashion. These trainers are experts at knowing when to back off work loads and judge the condition of their horses.

*** The heavy in condition type, with muscle definition around 75% and plenty of rib cage cover. This style always gives me the impression they are a race or gallop short, and I subsequently marked them accordingly, but plenty of trainers consistently turn their horses out this way. It was always noteworthy, with sometimes good results, when a trainer in this category paraded a runner with a more tightened appearance.

*** The blank appearance. Not a lot of muscle definition, plain muscle bulk and structure. They generally look like they're "coming along" OK but are only around the 75% fit stage. These usually slot into the "Average" fitness category.

*** The very lean, light, angular look. A very old school style that I referred to as the hammered, hunted or greyhound look. For me they always went in the "Thin" fitness basket. Small muscle mass, slight hip protrusion, hollow flanks, lean neck and angular rear end. Even though that description doesn't seem apt for an equine athlete I do still see them repeatedly from some stables although not as much these days.

Along with fitness styles I've found many stables have horses that parade with distinct behavioural patterns.

*** Calm and compliant demeanour. Always easy to manage and parade.
*** Unruly, very difficult to lead.
*** Sweating, jig jogging and head tossing, projecting a nervous, anxious disposition.

Also, the ability of stables and trainers to regularly parade horses within certain profiles is determined by many factors.

*** Their yearling purchasing power. Top stables with big clients have access to the better quality animals, which in turn enables the trainer to acquire their preferred yearling type and hence contribute to the makeup of the stable "parade style".
*** The conditioning regimen the trainer applies.
*** The environment the horse resides in. Stabled. Paddocked.
*** The facilities available for training, such as, swimming pools, treadmills, hill gallops, water walkers etc.

As with everything to do with horses and racing, there are always exceptions to the rule. Naturally not every horse fits into a stable's general horse style, but with experience and good observation the yard analyst can begin to determine and identify what the trainer is trying to achieve with each horse, and this can create an opportunity and betting advantage.

The previously mentioned scenario where the stable has them heavy in condition and suddenly appears with a runner tightened right up. Or the top trainer who likes to have them wound up to rock hard fitness, parades one heavy in condition. Then the trainer whose horses tend to be very difficult to manage and sweat and jig jog, produce a calm compliant one. With the watcher having the ability to identify these situations it provides an insight that other punters may not have and is another factor that can join the myriads of factors that determine a wagering decision.

Also, if the yard analyst can identify these physical and mental variables that pertain consistently to certain stables, they can be well assured, that they have reached an advanced stage in their horse watching journey.

Wet Tracks

To be honest, I've never been able to identify any particular trait from the yard, that would consistently suggest it provided a pointer to a racehorse that was more likely to handle, or even excel, on a rain affected track, and I've tried a few. There well maybe an indicator out there but I've abandoned that pursuit and left the possible answer to the past performance form guide and the breeding. Especially when there are so many variations in the types of rain affected tracks. Deep, gluey or sticky, wet and splashy, sandy, loamy and just plain slippery to name a few. On top of that, a horse may excel on a sandy heavy and perform poorly on a gluey heavy.

Chapter 21. Factor Discussion, Tables and Combinations

There was a suggestion that hoof size was a factor. The larger hoof wouldn't penetrate the ground as much and the smaller hoof would spear further in and take longer to pull out, hence slowing down the stride rate. I collected some data on that but couldn't make head nor tail out of it. Similarly, there was the theory of the lighter body type being able to skip through the conditions more easily than the heavier robust type, only to see on as many occasions the robust type use its strength to power through the ground, with the lighter type tiring badly.

I also looked at the possibility that horses with long walking extensions may become unbalanced in affected going, so I collected overstep measurements in the parade ring, but no joy there either. Admittedly, not a large amount of data was collected, and it could be classified as "one rat research", but I felt there was enough for a trend to begin to appear, so as previously stated, for me, it's best left up to what the horse has displayed in its previous performances and the statistical tendencies of the breed.

Chapter 22. Actual v Expected – The A/E Index

A/E Description

In this chapter I'll delve into some "end game" questions as to why one would want to take on the pursuit of developing the ability to assess a racehorse pre-race.

    How do we know if we have an edge?
    How do we identify it?
    How do we give it a value?
    Can we profit from it?

Firstly, a couple of things to remember here. I am by no means an expert in statistics or data science, just an average long-term punter and I'm sure those educated in those subjects would have deeper methods they'd prefer to use, but for this exercise, for us average punters, the metric used should suffice and offer us a window into knowing where we stand regarding having an edge or not. Like the Impact Values used for the factor descriptions, the metric used here is based on "my" identification of the variables at the yard. As I've previously stated, if one has an aptitude for good observation and has studied the factor descriptions, then the variation between my results and another yard watcher's results shouldn't vary that much, therefore the figures provided here shouldn't deviate a great deal from one's own either.

So far, the metric used to evaluate factor strength has been the Impact Value (IV). Whilst it is a very powerful and important figure, showing one whether groups of horses with a particular factor are winning more than their relative share of races, it doesn't tell us if one can have a betting advantage or profit return, from wagering on the factors. For that, one can use the efficiency of the market and the odds within the market to try and gauge if there is an edge. The metric used for this purpose is the "A/E Index". It's also commonly referred to as "Actual V Expected", "A/E Ratio", "A/E Value Indicator", but for reference here I'll just go with the simpler "A/E".

The formula for the A/E is the number of actual winners divided by the expected number of winners.

The actual winners are simply the number of those that won with the factor being evaluated. The expected number of wins is where the market comes in and for this the odds probabilities for each horse, with the factor, are summed.

    Eg. If a horse is $4 its probability is 0.25 (1 divided by 4). This is done for each horse and the sum of the probabilities is the expected number of wins. This expected number of wins is then divided into the actual figure, to return the A/E, which may be above or below 1, like the IV.

(The resultant A/Es in Table 10 are after a 7% commission was accounted for. Betfair Exchange commissions may be less or more elsewhere.)

As an example, from Table 10 I'll use variable 34 – Fat.
    5612 were in the Fat category
    180 actual winners
    281 was the expected number from summing the probabilities
    So, 180 divided by 281 (actual/expected) = A/E 0.64

Using factor 15 "Ground Licker" as another example.
    505 were Ground Lickers
    85 actual winners
    79 were expected to win
    A/E = 1.08 (85 divided by 79)

Chapter 22. Actual v Expected – The A/E Index

With this Ground Licker result one can interpret it as saying that if each horse was backed a profit of 8% could be made, even after the 7% Exchange commission. The conclusion may also be drawn that the factor is under bet in the market and the A/E has shown us where an edge, or advantage wager may prevail. Knowing the A/E value cuts through all the discussion and banter around yard analyst's opinions on what is a good factor or not and what is good or poor value. One must also remember that this can all be flipped over, and the poor A/E values utilised on the "Lay" side, for those with betting exchange access.

Table 10 – A/E Index Values

- Note – All odds used in Table 10 are real time odds, taken when the horses were behind the barrier. They are not Betfair SP.
- 7% commission was accounted for in the win component when evaluating the A/E. This may vary according to racing jurisdiction.
- The second last column of the table looks at horses under $11 or "in the market" to gauge market influences on the A/E value.

No.	Factor	Count	A/E	Rank	Count	A/E <= $11	Rank
1	Facial Expressions	286	0.81	30	98	0.73	46
2	Ears Pricked	930	0.88	23	570	0.92	20
3	Ears Negative	562	0.81	30	143	0.88	24
4	Bit Play	4511	0.94	15	1938	1.00	10
5	Bit Grinding	160	0.80	33	59	0.75	44
6	Salivate Mild	816	0.97	10	373	1.02	9
7	Salivate Heavy	80	0.89	21	0	0.00	53
8	Still Mouth	972	1.14	2	274	1.13	3
9	Head Toss	1306	0.73	43	478	0.79	37
10	Neck Positive	1275	0.93	16	964	0.92	20
11	Neck Negative	267	0.67	50	97	0.84	28
12	Neck Arched	743	0.97	10	413	1.00	10
13	Neck Twisted	622	1.09	4	339	1.14	2
14	Neck Horizontal	508	0.85	25	260	0.87	25
15	Ground Licker	505	1.08	5	330	1.07	4
16	Shoulder Positive	2571	0.84	27	1984	0.84	28
17	Rib Cage Positive	2767	0.83	28	2249	0.83	31
18	Rib Cage Negative	8941	0.75	38	4080	0.78	40
19	Tension Line	1386	0.77	37	477	0.77	41
20	Underbelly Negative	4980	0.69	48	1008	0.77	41
21	Flanks Negative	2188	0.70	47	799	0.71	48
22	Money Mark Positive	3869	0.80	33	2738	0.80	35
23	Money Mark Negative	5232	0.72	44	2046	0.75	44
24	Racing Dimple Positive	9425	0.82	29	7139	0.83	31
25	Racing Dimple Negative	637	0.74	40	245	0.85	27
26	Rump Top Negative	1090	0.71	45	293	0.69	51
27	Hip Pointing	4450	0.71	45	1622	0.73	46
28	Thigh Negative	3304	0.68	49	241	0.84	28

No.	Factor	Count	A/E	Rank	Count	A/E <= $11	Rank
29	Rump Top Positive	1547	0.97	10	1305	0.97	15
30	Tail Swishing	1787	0.95	14	714	0.96	16
31	Tail Jammed	297	1.03	8	85	1.04	7
32	Fit	8689	0.92	18	3676	0.99	12
33	Average	14993	0.79	36	5658	0.80	35
34	Fat	5612	0.64	52	643	0.70	49
35	Thin	2685	0.64	51	496	0.70	49
36	Power Walk	5422	0.96	13	3152	0.95	18
37	Walking Short	4592	0.74	40	2019	0.79	37
38	Jig Jogging	4390	0.75	38	1935	0.79	37
39	Double Tracking	578	1.08	5	161	1.06	5
40	Scuffing	91	0.59	53	0	0.00	53
41	Focus/Transition	592	1.12	3	312	1.06	5
42	Behaviour Negative	1403	0.74	40	425	0.81	34
43	Glowing Coat	768	0.98	9	454	0.99	12
44	Dappled Coat	501	0.92	18	263	0.99	12
45	Dull Coat	478	0.80	33	121	0.86	26
46	Bum Sweat	1189	0.93	16	558	0.96	16
47	Body Sweat	2502	0.89	21	892	0.91	23
48	Size Big	666	0.92	18	304	0.95	18
49	Size Small	207	0.87	24	73	0.77	41
50	Droppings Loose	413	1.06	7	244	1.04	7
51	Droppings Firm	738	0.85	25	297	0.92	20
52	Groom Negative	164	0.81	30	72	0.83	31
53	Canter Off Positive	682	1.20	1	293	1.24	1
54	Canter Off Negative	741	0.58	54	321	0.61	52

Generally, the factor strength trends of the A/E values tend to follow those of the IV's. Looking at Table 11, an Impact Value and A/E comparison there is a change in the make-up of the A/E top five, as the fitness variables from the IV's, Rump Top Positive and Fit, have dropped out. They remain very strong figures, but their departure may be due to market awareness of a horse's fitness stage through stable information or past performance factors and are hence fully accounted for in the market odds. On the other hand, those in the top 5 A/E for overall and under $11 are all factors that wouldn't be frequently identified by most horse watchers and are therefore under bet in the market.

Table 11 – Impact Value and A/E Comparison of Top 5 Variables

No.	IV Factor	Value	A/E Factor	Value	A/E <=$11	Value
1	Focus/Trans	3.06	Canter Off	1.2	Canter Off	1.24
2	Rump Top Pos	2.31	Still Mouth	1.14	Neck Twist	1.14
3	Canter Off	2.1	Focus/Trans	1.12	Still Mouth	1.13
4	Fit	2.09	Neck Twist	1.09	Ground Licker	1.07
5	Still Mouth	1.96	Ground Licker	1.08	Focus/Trans	1.06
=5			Double Track	1.08	Double Track	1.06

Chapter 21. Factor Discussion, Tables and Combinations

The A/E Index puts one in a better position to know when there may be an edge, or advantage in a wagering market. Instead of working off personal assumptions or preferences of what a factor's value may be, one can factually know what they are dealing with. Most of the operators I've dealt with, from track walkers to sectional time gurus, don't go by impressions, they want to know what the reality is. Data and figures. As markets evolve, so will the A/E values, and this applies to horse watching values too, so it's important if you're a collector of watching data to keep up to date and know where you stand.

Factor Combinations and the A/E Index

The following combination tables are broken down into two fitness categories, Fit and Average, and then matched with other positive and negative variables. Only those with reliable count numbers were included as there was a total of 4377 combinations in the data, with the majority of those thinning out into small numbers.

The Fat and Thin fitness categories were not used as the numbers were depleted somewhat and adding positives didn't increase the A/E at all and the addition of negative variables just sent the A/E out the back door. The values are all based on the overall A/E and no odds brackets were included.

Table 12 – A/E Index Values of Fit and Positive Variables

The values in brackets next to the factors are those of the Overall A/E from Table 10, included here for comparison with the combination values.

Factor Combinations		Count	A/E Value
Fit (.92)	Ears Pricked (.88)	245	1.01
Fit (.92)	Still Mouth (1.14)	112	1.29
Fit (.92)	Neck Arched (.97)	156	1.21
Fit (.92)	Neck Twisted (1.09)	117	1.08
Fit (.92)	Ground Licker (1.08)	140	1.29
Fit (.92)	Power Walk (.96)	523	1.01
Fit (.92)	Double Tracking (1.08)	95	1.16
Fit (.92)	Focus/Transition (1.12)	261	1.09
Fit (.92)	Glowing Coat (.98)	311	.86
Fit (.92)	Dappled Coat (.92)	115	.84
Fit (.92)	Droppings Loose (1.06)	111	.93
Fit (.92)	Canter Off Positive (1.2)	154	1.16

The general trend from Table 12 is that the individual A/E values were elevated and, in some cases, quite substantially. This highlights the advantage of being capable of identifying a fit racehorse with other positive characteristics. The exceptions to this trend were with the two coat categories, Glowing and Dappled. A possible reason is that they are easily recognised, even by the novice, and that may flow through to causing a diminished A/E value due to them being over bet in the market.

The takeaway from the figures is that, like the Impact Values, the addition of a positive variable to a good fitness category increases the overall strength of each attribute in the combination and subsequently increases the strength of the A/E value.

Chapter 21. Factor Discussion, Tables and Combinations

Table 13 – A/E Index Values of Fit and Negative Variables

Factor Combinations		Count	A/E Value
Fit (.92)	Ears Negative (.81)	86	.62
Fit (.92)	Bit Play (.94)	692	1.02
Fit (.92)	Salivate Mild (.97)	131	.97
Fit (.92)	Head Toss (.73)	130	.92
Fit (.92)	Tension Line (.77)	168	.91
Fit (.92)	Tail Swishing (.95)	202	.68
Fit (.92)	Walking Short (.74)	138	.81
Fit (.92)	Jig Jogging (.75)	757	.84
Fit (.92)	Behaviour Negative (.74)	349	.99
Fit (.92)	Bum Sweat (.93)	209	.90
Fit (.92)	Body Sweat (.89)	238	.87
Fit (.92)	Droppings Firm (.85)	105	.98

This is an interesting table with the expectation being that the addition of a negative to the Fit category might see the power of a fit racehorse hold its ground and be able to offset any negativity. This was the case to some degree, with an increase even in a few factor combinations, but some had a large decrease in A/E values.

These were Ears Negative, Tail Swishing, Walking Short, Jig Jogging and Body Sweating. All variables that may be indicative of a sour, sore or irritated horse. Even though the horse was assessed as Fit, some underlying problem or environmental cause may be at play with the animal. This is an opening for the punter to slide in on the "Lay" side or drop the horse from their contenders. Especially with the Negative Ears and Tail Swishing variables that dropped to .62 and .68 A/E's respectively. An irritated horse? So going by these A/E values, long term "Laying" or backing avoidance of these combinations may be fruitful. The A/E index gives us an idea of where we stand in these situations.

Table 14 – A/E Index Values of Average and Positive Variables

Factor Combinations		Count	A/E Value
Average (.79)	Ears Pricked (.88)	661	.79
Average (.79)	Still Mouth (1.14)	152	1.10
Average (.79)	Neck Arched (.97)	566	.85
Average (.79)	Neck Twisted (1.09)	483	1.10
Average (.79)	Ground Licker (1.08)	350	1.06
Average (.79)	Power Walk (.96)	5625	.88
Average (.79)	Double Tracking (1.08)	311	.95
Average (.79)	Focus/Transition (1.12)	328	.98
Average (.79)	Glowing Coat (.98)	496	1.08
Average (.79)	Dappled Coat (.92)	354	.99
Average (.79)	Droppings Loose (1.06)	273	1.13
Average (.79)	Canter Off Positive (1.2)	89	1.22

Chapter 21. Factor Discussion, Tables and Combinations

Table 14 results look fairly self-explanatory with the strong variables asserting themselves on the combinations. The A/E values in this table actually make a case for one to dispense with trying to evaluate distinctions between "Fit" and "Average and look for these "power factors" on their own. This is discussed further in the chapter on "Using the Knowledge".

Table 15 – A/E Index Values of Average and Negative Variables

Factor Combinations		Count	A/E Value
Average (.79)	Ears Negative (.81)	464	.92
Average (.79)	Bit Play (.94)	3521	.90
Average (.79)	Salivate Mild (.97)	620	.97
Average (.79)	Head Toss (.73)	1090	.94
Average (.79)	Tension Line (.77)	676	.64
Average (.79)	Tail Swishing (.95)	1429	.73
Average (.79)	Walking Short (.74)	144	.99
Average (.79)	Jig Jogging (.75)	3851	.77
Average (.79)	Behaviour Negative (.74)	1831	.71
Average (.79)	Bum Sweat (.93)	1109	.98
Average (.79)	Body Sweat (.89)	2045	.96
Average (.79)	Droppings Firm (.85)	558	.80

A very mixed bag of A/E value results from the combination of Average and a negative variable. Only four combinations returned lower A/E's than the .79 of "Average". Quite a few increased in value and others stayed around the overall values of the negative component of the combination.

A contributing factor to some of the increases may be attributable to my categorisation of the fitness factor. Often when dealing with horses parading on the borderline of Fit and Average, where it is a close decision to call them Fit, I would tend to drop them down to the Average category, so a lot of winning chances would be in the Average class. Whether this is an influential component on the increases in A/E values, I'm not sure, but could be a reason. It's a fine line and one can't be correct in fitness decisions 100% of the time.

Distance and the A/E Index

The distance brackets used in Table 16 are the same as those used for the Impact Value distance effects in Table 2, Short, Mid and Long.

Column 3, A/E Index, is the value from Table 10, included here for comparison of the Overall A/E Index values with the distance values.

Table 16 – A/E Index Values of Short, Mid, Long Distances

Var.#	Factor	Overall A/E Index	Count	Short	Mid	Long
1	Facial Expressions	0.81	286	0.88	0.85	0.69
2	Ears Pricked	0.88	930	0.83	0.97	0.82
3	Ears Negative	0.81	562	1.10	0.64	0.68
4	Bit Play	0.94	4511	0.97	0.87	1.02

Chapter 21. Factor Discussion, Tables and Combinations

Var.#	Factor	Overall A/E Index	Count	Short	Mid	Long
5	Bit Grinding	0.80	160	1.01	0.63	0.76
6	Salivate Mild	0.97	816	1.03	0.96	0.80
7	Salivate Heavy	0.89	80	0.55	1.41	0.70
8	Still Mouth	1.14	972	1.05	1.08	1.22
9	Head Toss	0.73	1306	0.86	0.69	0.71
10	Neck Positive	0.93	1275	0.96	0.85	1.02
11	Neck Negative	0.67	267	0.50	0.98	0.61
12	Neck Arched	0.97	743	1.05	0.89	1.00
13	Neck Twisted	1.09	622	1.15	0.97	1.22
14	Neck Horizontal	0.85	508	0.74	0.90	0.98
15	Ground Licker	1.08	505	0.91	1.19	1.20
16	Shoulder Positive	0.84	2571	0.81	0.84	0.95
17	Rib Cage Positive	0.83	2767	0.80	0.80	0.91
18	Rib Cage Negative	0.75	8941	0.74	0.79	0.66
19	Tension Line	0.77	1386	0.78	0.90	0.63
20	Underbelly Negative	0.69	4980	0.76	0.58	0.78
21	Flanks Negative	0.70	2188	0.56	0.72	0.84
22	Money Mark Positive	0.80	3869	0.77	0.81	0.83
23	Money Mark Negative	0.72	5232	0.70	0.76	0.68
24	Racing Dimple Positive	0.82	9425	0.81	0.83	0.83
25	Racing Dimple Negative	0.74	637	0.83	0.64	0.75
26	Rump Top Negative	0.71	1090	0.57	0.67	0.82
27	Hip Pointing	0.71	4450	0.64	0.68	0.80
28	Thigh Negative	0.68	3304	0.41	0.78	0.77
29	Rump Top Positive	0.97	1547	0.97	0.97	1.00
30	Tail Swishing	0.95	1787	1.01	0.91	0.90
31	Tail Jammed	1.03	297	1.32	0.99	0.75
32	Fit	0.92	8689	0.84	0.97	0.96
33	Average	0.79	14993	0.76	0.78	0.79
34	Fat	0.64	5612	0.74	0.57	0.56
35	Thin	0.64	2685	0.50	0.71	0.67
36	Power Walk	0.96	5422	0.87	1.00	1.02
37	Walking Short	0.74	4592	0.76	0.74	0.66
38	Jig Jogging	0.75	4390	0.78	0.75	0.67
39	Double Tracking	1.08	578	1.17	0.99	1.06
40	Scuffing	0.59	91	0.69	0.76	0.38
41	Focus/Transition	1.12	592	1.09	1.03	1.18
42	Behaviour Negative	0.74	1403	0.86	0.73	0.69
43	Glowing Coat	0.98	768	1.10	0.88	0.89
44	Dappled Coat	0.92	501	0.93	0.96	0.82

Chapter 21. Factor Discussion, Tables and Combinations

Var.#	Factor	Overall A/E Index	Count	Short	Mid	Long
45	Dull Coat	0.80	478	0.81	0.66	0.92
46	Bum Sweat	0.93	1189	1.05	0.88	0.85
47	Body Sweat	0.89	2502	1.03	0.95	0.85
48	Size Big	0.92	666	1.08	0.68	1.14
49	Size Small	0.87	207	0.55	1.03	1.03
50	Droppings Loose	1.06	413	1.04	1.17	0.90
51	Droppings Firm	0.85	738	0.82	0.83	0.98
52	Groom Negative	0.81	164	0.87	0.74	0.83
53	Canter Off Positive	1.20	682	1.18	1.11	1.25
54	Canter Off Negative	0.58	741	0.69	0.59	0.59

Although there are some anomalies in the distance values in Table 16, (Salivate Heavy, Tail Jam, Size Small), most likely due to low count numbers in the distance brackets, there are clearly substantial changes in factor A/E values across the ranges. Some factors weaken with distance increases, while others strengthen, some remain much the same and a few remain variables that are just poor negatives wherever they may land. I'll firstly look at the variables that increase in A/E value from Short to Long.

Factor	Short – Long	Increase
Still Mouth	1.05 – 1.22	.17
Neck Twisted	1.15 – 1.22	.07
Neck Horizontal	.74 - .98	.24
Ground Licker	.91 – 1.20	.29
Power Walk	.87 – 1.02	.15
Focus/Transition	1.09 – 1.18	.09
Canter Off Positive	1.18 – 1.25	.07

There are some very large increases, and they highlight the attributes preferred for the longer distance style of horse and it's somewhat understandable why they increase. The Still Mouth factor means the horse is completely comfortable in the mouth and will more than likely race tractably for the rider with a good respiratory pattern. The Neck Twisted, Horizontal and Ground Licker factors, reinforce how important it is to observe good neck carriage in the parade ring.

The strong Power Walker implies that there will be no impediment to the stride of the horse, and it should stretch out well, as in the parade. The focused horse is in the zone, unphased feeling well and is at peace with what is coming and the same with the Canter Off Positive horse that slots into the profile and is in sync with the rider. Identifying this number one ranked variable is paramount as it is the last assessment we can make from a parade and the closest suggestion as to how the horse may perform.

The breakdown in distance has really made the attribute requirements of the staying horse obvious, and looking at that group of factors, coming across a horse now and then, carrying a few of the variables would be very rewarding. They constitute the perfect profile for a distance horse. I'll now have a look at the factors not wanted in the staying horse, those that decreased as the distance increased.

Factor	Short – Long	Decrease
Facial Expressions.	.88 - .69	.19
Ears Negative	1.1 - .68	.42

Chapter 21. Factor Discussion, Tables and Combinations

Factor	Short – Long	Decrease
Bit Grinding	1.01 - .76	.25
Salivate Mild	1.03 - .80	.23
Head Toss	.86 - .71	.15
Tension Line	.78 - .63	.15
Tail Swishing	1.01 - .90	.11
Tail Jammed	1.32 - .75	.57
Walking Short	.76 - .66	.10
Jig Jogging	.78 - .67	.11
Behaviour Negative	.86 - .69	.17
Bum Sweat	1.05 - .85	.20
Body Sweat	1.03 - .85	.18
Canter Off Negative	.69 - .59	.10

Just like the factors that increased in value and produced a clear picture of a good staying profile, the variables that decreased in value set a clear picture of the non-preferred attributes in the longer distance racehorse. All the variables point to a horse that is possibly experiencing some form of apprehension, nerves, soreness, irritability or the effect of the prevailing environmental conditions, such as heat or humidity. At the very least they are indicators of an unsettled or partially compromised horse, which is not the optimum state when contesting a race distance that requires tractability and energy preservation.

Turning now to the sprinters or short course races it is often heard said that some forgiveness or cutting of slack can be applied due to the nature and disposition of the sprinting horse. They are perceived as being generally more hyped up or reactionary compared to the more sedate nature of the distance horse. The following group of factors looks at the validity of this assumption by comparing negative factor values to the Overall A/E from the third column of Table 16.

Factor	Overall A/E to Short	Increase/Decrease
Facial Expressions.	.81 - .88	.07
Ears Negative	.81 – 1.10	.29
Bit Play	.94 - .97	.03
Bit Grinding	.80 – 1.01	.21
Head Toss	.73 - .86	.13
Tension Line	.77 - .78	.01
Tail Swish	.95 – 1.01	.06
Tail Jammed	1.03 – 1.32	.29
Walking Short	.74 - .76	.02
Jig Jogging	.75 - .78	.03
Behaviour Negative	.74 - .86	.12
Dull Coat	.80 - .81	.01
Bum Sweat	.93 – 1.05	.12
Body Sweat	.89 – 1.03	.14
Canter Off Negative	.58 - .69	.11

The resultant A/E values show that all the differences actually increase from the Overall A/E to the Short category, some minimally and some still staying well below the "break even" figure of one. The latter maintain their status as being a poor attribute no matter what the situation may be.

In trying to draw an acceptable profile from these figures for the sprinting horse, I would suggest that some Body Sweat and Bum Sweat is reasonable, along with some bit chewing and intermittent Tail Swishing and laying back of the ears. These factors would need to be accompanied by a reasonable walk and free of any negative behaviour, head tossing or Tension Line with a close watch of the Canter Off.

As for the four fitness categories, they decreased in this comparison with the exception of "Fat" that had an increase of .10, from .64 to .74, which still remains a very negative figure. Also, the factors that comprised the preferred profile of the staying type, all held their ground at the Short category, proving their strength in any set of race circumstances.

A/E Index Summary

In this chapter the endeavour was to add some profitability expectations of the factors for the punter/yard assessor, through use of the A/E Index.

We've looked at the Overall A/E value and then broken it down into distance influences, market influences and what affect negative and positive factor additions have on the "Fit" and "Average" categories. The purpose of all this is so the horse watcher can be at the yard and have confidence in knowing where they stand regarding the prevailing race conditions. Familiarity of the A/E tables provides knowledge of a "profit profile" so to speak, of the current race conditions, be that distance, market rank, or weather conditions. The A/E values, along with the Impact Values, allow an insight into what's "real" regarding horse factors. This creates a strong base of knowledge to start with before a horse has even entered the parade ring. What factors are good and bad, what to look for and awareness of the preferred profile to match the conditions.

Chapter 23. "At The Parade"

In this chapter we look at the practicalities and vagaries of being at the racecourse and utilising the horse watching descriptions and factors to hopefully find a betting edge.

Access and Positioning

The layouts of most racecourses that I've been to, both here in Australia and overseas, all appear very similar. There's the stalls area where the horses are kept, a pre-parade ring nearby for walking the horses and the main mounting yard, or paddock enclosure, where the horses are paraded before the jockeys mount up and head out onto the course.

One thing that may vary is access to the stalls area and pre-parade ring. Not all tracks allow access and the watcher in that case is restricted to the main parade ring. In Australia there is public access to the main ring at all tracks and usually no problems taking up one's favoured position on the fence. I found in Asia that the main parade rings are often at the rear of the grandstands, and you need to get there early, as viewing the horses is hugely popular and there can be thousands taking up vantage points on main race days.

One of the factors worth taking note of in the stalls area is the acceptance of the horse to being saddled. Where stalls access is restricted that is not possible, but in some jurisdictions the horses are saddled in areas adjacent to the main parade enclosure and the yard analyst can take advantage of viewing this.

As far as positioning at the parade ring is concerned, my preference is to view from the long side of the yard, if there is one, with the sun behind me if possible and try to avoid standing at the corners. I prefer to be able to view the longest section across the other side of the yard where I can assess the horses' walks better from a bit of distance, rather than being close up to me on the near side. Regular parade ring attendees will eventually find their preferred spot and it's common to find the same racegoers, in the same positions, at all the different tracks one goes to.

Viewing Procedure

This is the viewing pattern I adopted over time and tried to adhere to this same routine on every horse that paraded. I found the repetitiveness meant each horse got a good viewing and I wasn't jumping all over the place from one horse to the other. It leads to consistency and the likelihood one won't miss noticing some

Chapter 23. "At The Parade"

factors.

If stalls and pre-parade ring access is available, I would browse through there and note any poor behaviour such as difficult walkers for the handler, kicking out in the stalls and pawing the ground. If the saddling procedure is viewable, I would be looking for signs of resentment and annoyance, just getting a feel for some of the competitors prior to their main assessment in the parade ring.

Often the initial look we get of the horses is their entry into the main yard enclosure. Entry here marks a transitional point for them, as they are in a new environment that may have more noise, people and other distractions. At this point I'm looking to see how they react to the change. Are they sensible about entering? No hesitation? Or are they anxious? The factors here to note would be, Focus/Transition, ear position, facial expressions and behaviour. At this stage I wouldn't be setting factor decisions in concrete, unless they were obvious or severe. A case in point is the jig jogger. If a horse breaks into a reasonably tame jig jog, I will give it a half a lap or so to see if it continued to do it, as it's quite common for a horse to get up on its toe for a short time when changing environments.

As the horses approach me, I'm assessing their head virtually front on, noting facial expressions, still mouth, nostril shapes, mouth saliva, bit play and ear position. Then as they begin to become side on to me, I'm looking for muscle bulk and definition, body sweat, bum sweat and tail carriage. Firstly, the neck for shape, strength and definition, the same with the shoulder, then the mid-section, underbelly and rib cage, followed most importantly by the rear end. Here I check for hip pointing, muscle definitions, shape and strength again and particularly the rump top. I like to view it from a 45-degree angle as it walks away from me, checking if there is "build" above the hip and good strong muscle development over the top.

As the horse walks down the long section of the yard, on the other side, I can assess the walking action, as it is difficult when they are closer to me on the near side. From across the ring, I can profile the various neck carriages, coat conditions, head tossing, tail position and size. During the parade I'm always noting things such as, groom behaviour, droppings and negative behavioural factors. After taking all this in, at this point I've usually formed an assessment on fitness and can begin to slot each horse into their respective fitness categories of, fit, fat, average or thin.

The next part of the yard watch is the rider mounting and then the exit out onto the track. Here I'm looking for any resentment when the rider gets on board, such as swinging away, running forward or any noticeable dipping of the back, indicating possible soreness. As they exit on to the course, particular attention is paid to the canter off profile, as it is the strongest factor. A thing to note is, I never assess any factors after the riders have mounted, unless it's the canter off or a behavioural factor such as rider resentment. All the fitness assessments are prior to mounting, as I feel a lot of horses tighten up in appearance when first being ridden, possibly causing a false critique.
Two other things that one may encounter, is the horse that comes in late and gets taken straight out without being able to be viewed. That one's very annoying. Secondly there may be occasions in cold weather where the horse is rugged until the jockey gets legged up. This creates incomplete viewing of the horse and hence it's unwise to make a fitness call on it, but other factors can still be assessed, and one may choose to rely on those in this scenario.

Mind Games

A lot of thoughts go through a punter's mind when they're studying the form, on the racecourse, talking to others and weighing up wagering decisions. Doing pre-race fitness assessments is no different, and as a professional horse watcher for many years, with large amounts of money being turned over on what I was advising, it was necessary to provide clear, accurate information, and here are some of the tools and actions I took to ensure that.

I would print off a list of the races and runners for the day, but generally not look at it until the horses were entering the parade enclosure. People would ask what I liked for the day, and my response of telling them I hadn't looked at who was running was always met with an odd stare. I could sense what they were thinking. Here's this bloke working for the biggest wagering operation, and he doesn't even know who's running. Always amusing. Same result for the common question of, how does the favourite look? With the reply of, Who's the favourite? They were basically just all saddlecloth numbers to me, and I never really used horses' names. A running joke when walking off course was to try and name the winner of one of the races, I usually failed unless it was a well-known horse.

Maintain a positive attitude and clear head. Attend the paddock enclosure thinking you're going to find an edge or two. They're usually there, whether they are back opportunities or lay opportunities. The edge you find may simply be to not bet too, sometimes nothing seems to come at you. Don't force it, it may break. Shed any biases for jockeys, trainers or horses. We all have opinions on jockeys, stables and even favourite horses, but none of that is relevant at the yard. Be clinical in calling factors as you see them.

Separate yard assessing from form study. It's obviously very disheartening to spend hours studying race past performances, sectional times, speed maps and weights, and coming up with a possible strong wager, only to go to the yard and find it's a blithering mess. Lightened off, sweating, head tossing and jig jogging. Take it as a win. Money saved. I've come across many punters with the ability to talk themselves into saying "it should be OK, it's not too bad".

Handle distractions. Over the years I've come to recognise and encounter a lot of events that can be distracting while you're working a parade. Here's a few.

> The yapper or urger who's in your ear wanting to know what you think. Best thing is to tip them a loser, you probably won't hear from them again. But leave town if it gets up and wins.

> You've been given some red-hot stable information. Ignore.

> Media mounting yard person saying something is good or bad. Respect but ignore.

> Others' opinions. Respect but ignore.

> On course announcer saying a particular horse is being pounded in the betting. Ignore.

So, know your variables and how to identify them, back yourself, ignore outside influences and you'll more than likely be ahead of the crowd.

Put blinkers on at the yard and pacifiers on at bet decision time.

Chapter 24. "Parade Transcripts"

In this chapter I'll go through a pair of races that I marked, to give the reader an insight into my assessments. I'm aware that it's not ideal to work off a photo, as many of the markings won't be visible, but it should provide enough information for one to evaluate a reasonable assessment of some factors and compare those evaluations with my variables.

Both races were from a mid-week meeting in Melbourne, Australia and these meetings are generally considered second tier quality behind the stronger fields of Saturday and Public Holiday meetings. Nevertheless, many quality horses come through the ranks at these meetings on their way to higher quality races.

Parade (1)

This race was a 1200m Maiden for 3-year-olds in late winter.

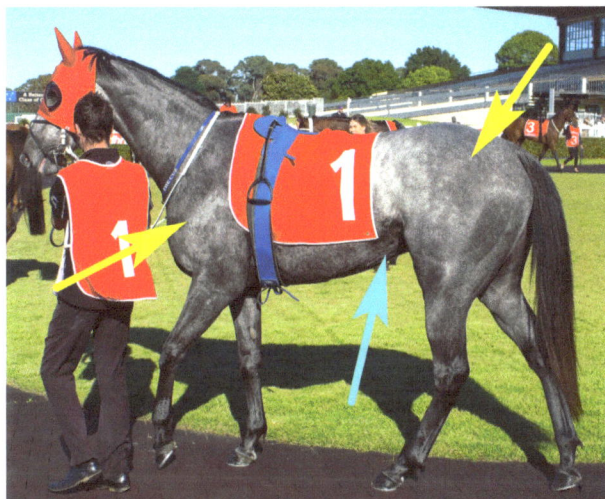

Horse #1   Odds $17

My immediate impression was that it wasn't a robust type and lacked some muscle definition, appearing blank through the shoulder and hindquarters. (Yellow Arrows). On that basis I gave it an "Average" fitness score.
It was also marked for Body Sweat around the flanks (Blue Arrow) and Bum Sweat, which developed during the parade. There was no positive or negative influence in either the walk, or behaviourally, so no further markings were applied.

Horse #3   Odds $6.5

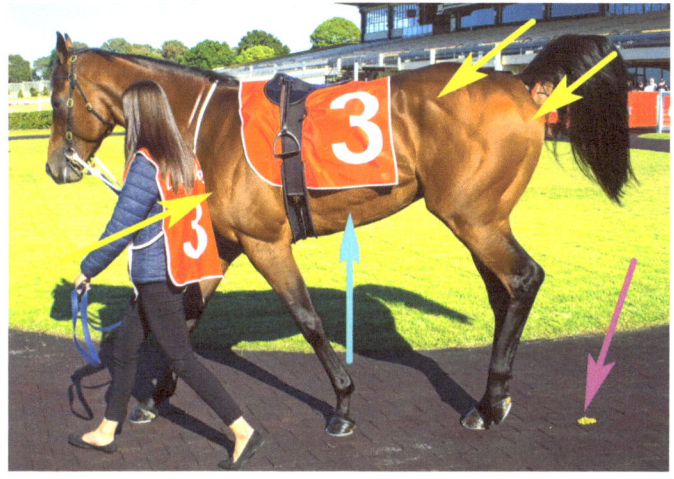

Straight away the muscle definition is noticeable. From the shoulder to the Money Mark, Racing Dimple and the roundness of the hindquarters, (Yellow Arrows) all depicting positive development and hence a "Fit" assessment. No Tension Line variable was allotted, (Blue Arrow), as this was attributable to the horse Dropping Loose (Pink Arrow), at the moment of capture. With the Glowing Coat and muscle presentation, this horse exudes a hint of quality.

Chapter 24. "Parade Transcripts"

Horse #4   Odds $6.5

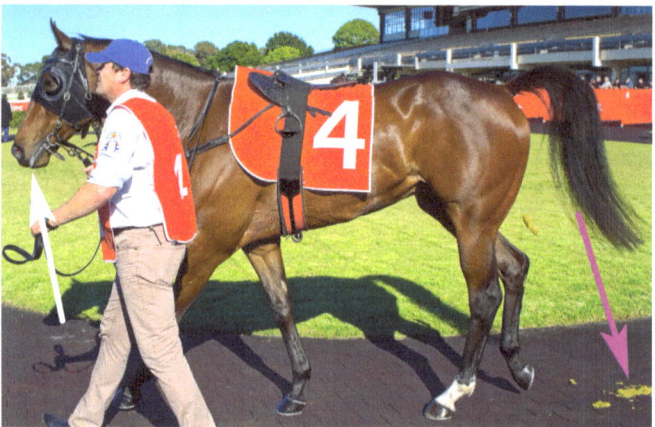

Horse 4 was, for my eye, at about 80% muscle definition, after coming off a long break. He had clearly done a lot of work for his return, but I thought he would improve from this run, so I put him in the "Average" fitness bracket.

He was further marked for Salivate Mild (White Arrow), Bit Play, Droppings Loose (Pink Arrow) and a Glowing Coat. Unfortunately, he also received a Canter Off Negative, which on the figures, virtually puts him out of contention.

Horse #5   Odds $10

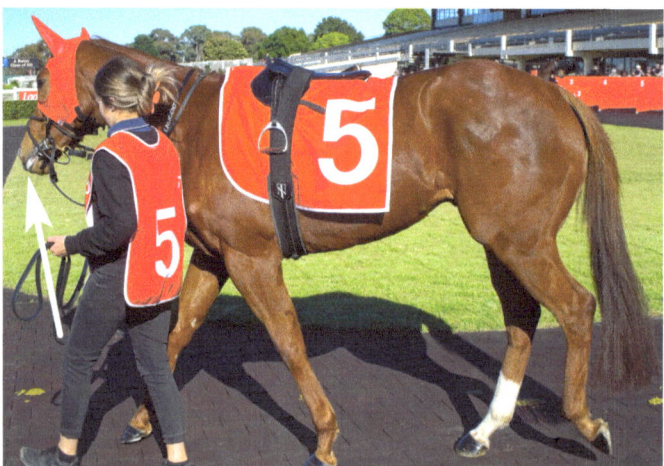

Horse 5 is a good example of looking beyond the rough winter coat and at the underlying muscles. He was assessed as Average fitness, but you could see that he was coming along well, with the definitions and shapes starting to appear under the long coat. He received a Salivate Mild and Bit Play also. (White Arrow). Behaviour and walk were basic, and he gave the impression that he was comfortable being there.

Horse #6   Odds $7

I marked Horse 6 Average for fitness, but he was borderline going into the Thin category. Forward of the saddle, in the shoulder and neck region, he had quite good development. Well defined and muscled for a leaner type. (Yellow Arrows). Whereas behind the saddle, he appeared hollow in the flanks (Pink Arrow) and the hip had slight pointing, (Blue Arrow), for which he was marked. Bit Play and Tail Swishing were further markings.

Chapter 24. "Parade Transcripts"

Horse #7   Odds $21

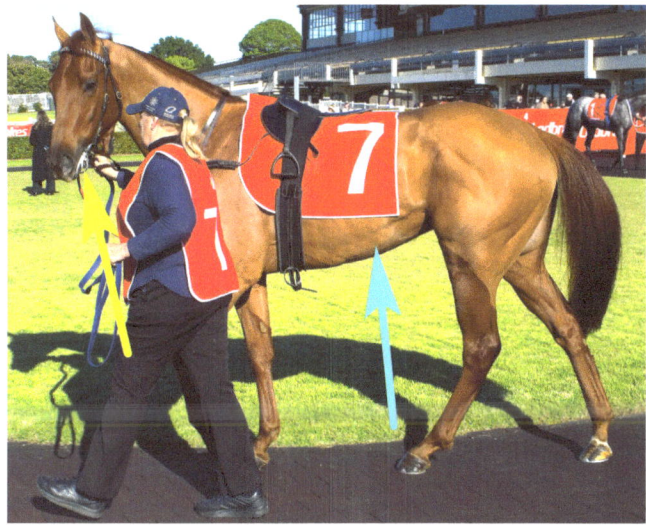

Horse 7 received an Average for fitness, even though the picture depicts him as being defined. He had a lot of apprehension about him, and the tightness was due more to that possibly, with his Jig Jogging, Bit Play, Salivation (Yellow Arrow) and the Tension Line (Blue Arrow) that was evident for the entire parade. He was intermittently Tail Swishing and Head tossing too, all signs that he may have been concerned with the proceedings.

Horse #8   Odds $2.7

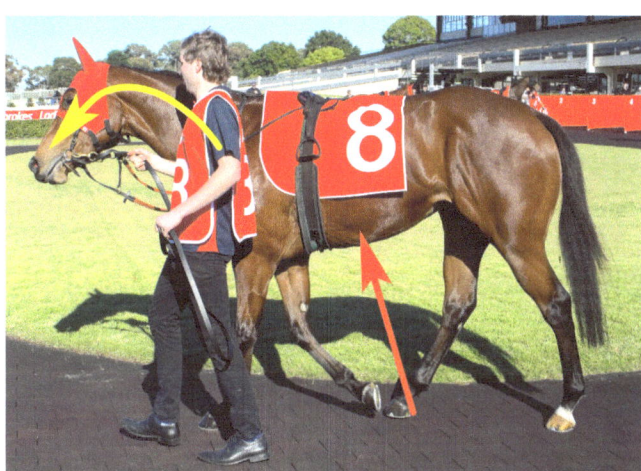

This horse received a "Fit" even though the picture makes it look like there is excess condition around the rib cage and underbelly, below the saddlecloth. That wasn't the case, it's due to the posture captured. There was great muscle definition, with a rich coat and the very high rated Twisted Neck attribute. Small Bum Sweat developed but no negatives observed, and this was a good parade from a horse at ease with her surroundings.

Horse #9   Odds $61

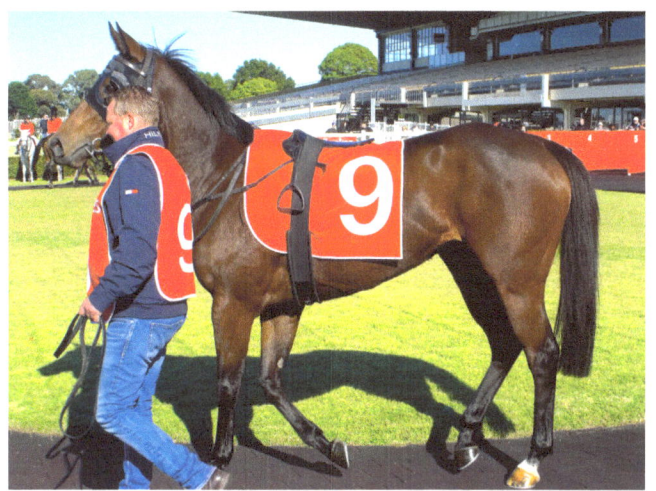

Horse 9 was a first starter, immediately recognisable as being a bit "new". The filly was light in muscle development, both bulk and definition, whilst displaying Head Tossing and Bit Play and intermittently breaking into a Jig Jog. All things one may expect from a first starter. She didn't completely lose the plot, as some can do, just a display of variables to suggest she would benefit from the experience.

Chapter 24. "Parade Transcripts"

Horse #10   Odds $7

This was a very nice filly who paraded with some good attributes. She had a good coat, alert ears (Yellow Arrow), a horizontal neck carriage and was the best walker in the field.
I wrangled with the decision to mark her Fit or Average. I decided on the latter as she was still slightly undefined, particularly behind, (Red Arrows) and had some softness still to her muscle structure. Unfortunately, she went amiss in the race and was eased down.

Results -   Winner - Horse 8   Second - Horse 5   Third - Horse 1

Parade (2)

This race was a 1600 metre (8 furlong) Benchmark 70 Handicap.

Horse #1   Odds $5

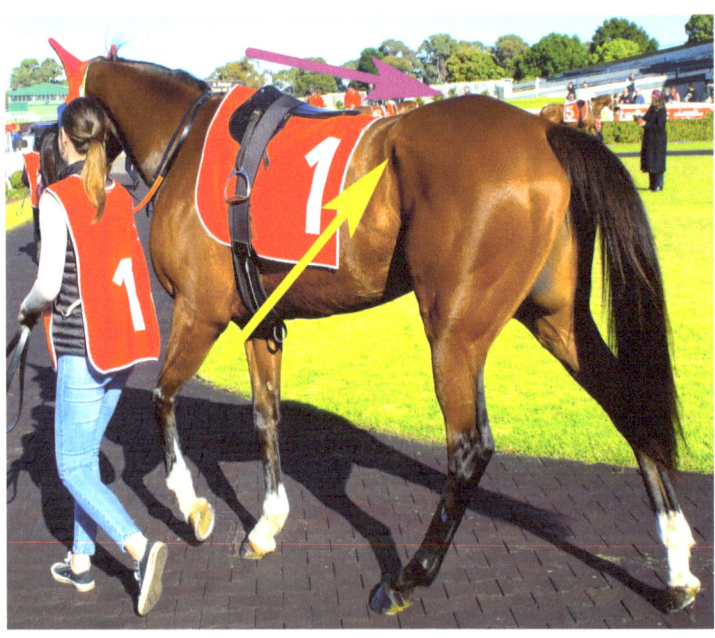

I gave Horse 1 a "Thin" for fitness as I thought he was starting to become depleted over the rear end. His hip was pointing (Yellow Arrow) and he was angular over the rump top (Pink Arrow). He was Jig Jogging consistently during the parade and chomping on the Bit excessively too. Forward of the saddle through the shoulder and neck he was actually fairly well muscled, as the picture shows, but as I have previously mentioned, as soon as I see a hip beginning to protrude, it gets marked harshly. For me, hip point equals turning point. I'm aware that some horses may have slight hip protrusion naturally through their conformation, but as it is difficult to recall every horses' status on this, I marked each horse as they appeared without trying to interpret what their conformation contributed to the decision. The poor Impact Values and A/E metrics probably justify my calling it as they appear in the parade. His markings were, Rump Top Negative, Hip Pointing, Thin, Bit Play and Jig Jogging.

Chapter 24. "Parade Transcripts"

Horse #2   Odds $9

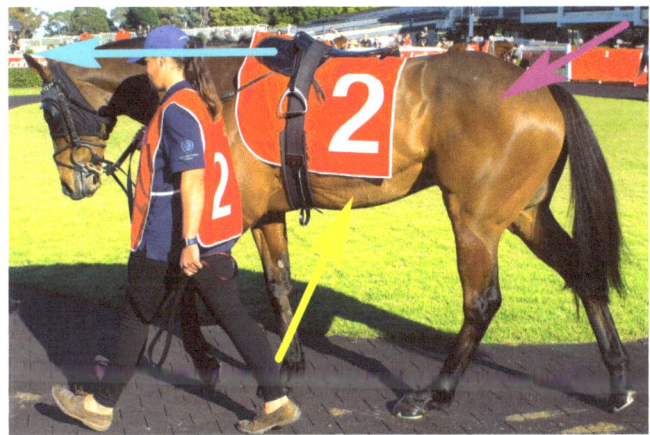

Horse #2 was marked as Average fitness as he was still relatively plain for muscle definition in the rear end (Pink Arrow) and shoulder region. I assessed him as coming along but benefitting from this race.

The only negative was the Tension Line (Yellow Arrow). He was very compliant with the groom and had a very good horizontal neck carriage (Blue Arrow).

Horse #3   Odds $5

Horse #3 was a bit of a mixed bag, with a very strong positive and a strong negative. He was a nice flowing Power Walker with a horizontal neck carriage, but I fitness categorised him as Thin.

The shoulder lacked bulk and definition (Blue Arrow) and there was Hip Pointing (Pink Arrow) and a rump top that was light and tended to fall away from the spine. (Yellow Arrows).

Horse #4   Odds $12

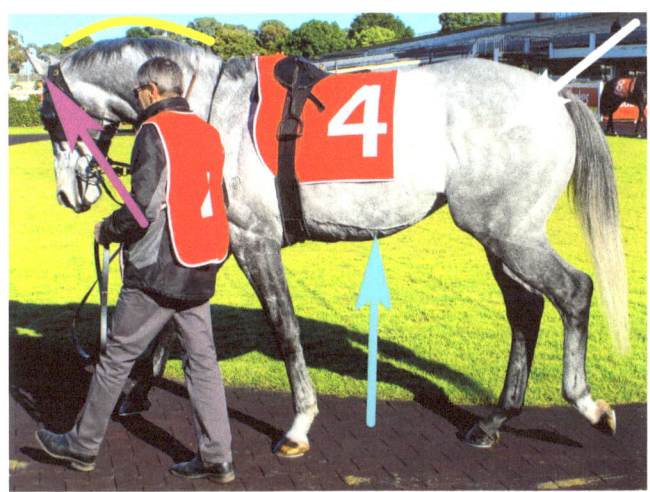

This horse was assessed as Fat due to the rib cage and underbelly condition coverage, (Blue Arrow) along with the lack of definition behind the saddle. (White Arrow). He also reefed and tossed his head at the Canter Off so received a Negative for that too.

He had some good attributes, with the Arched Neck (Yellow Marker) and very alert forward pointing ears. (Pink Arrow)

Chapter 24. "Parade Transcripts"

Horse #5   Odds $4.60

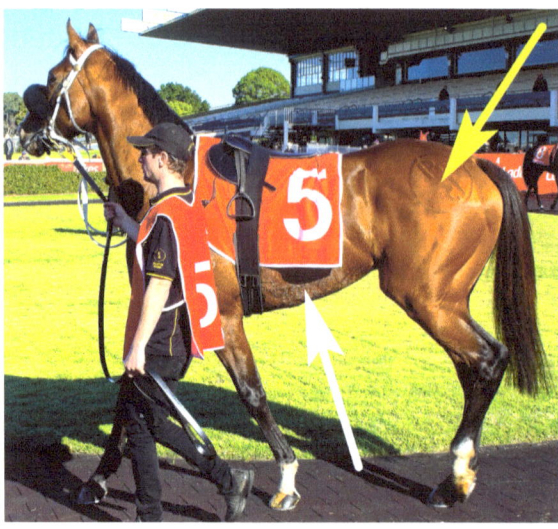

Horse #5 was a very lean type that I gave an Average fitness classification to. There was no evidence of hip protrusion, and the muscle definition was coming through in the rear end, (Yellow Arrow) although is somewhat accentuated in the picture due to the flexed position of that near hind leg.

The coat had a nice glow, but there was increasing Body Sweat, (White Arrow), Bum Sweat and a propensity to toss the head up.

Horse #6   Odds $8.50

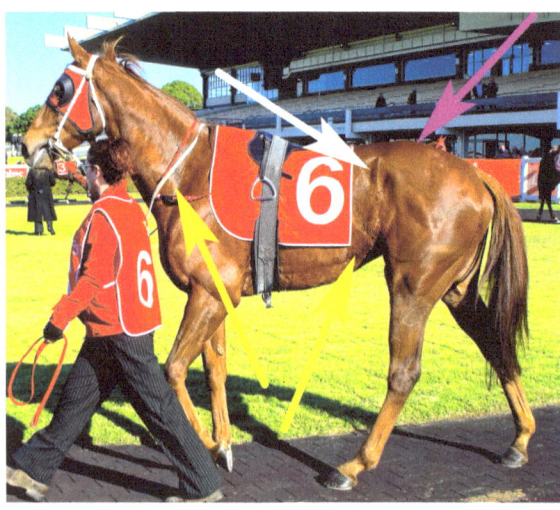

Horse #6 may be the victim of having a wintery coat in the sunshine, as the Body Sweat (Yellow Arrows) over the neck and flanks would indicate. He also developed some Bum Sweat during the course of the parade.

Fitness wise, he was another that I marked Thin, due to the Hip Pointing (White Arrow) and the slight falling away over the top of the rump. (Pink Arrow). He was borderline to be categorised as Average fitness but with the hip exposure I tend to drop them into the lower fitness class.
He was also very playful with the bit in his mouth and subsequently developed some mild salivation around the lips, that is evident in the picture.

Horse #7   Odds $20

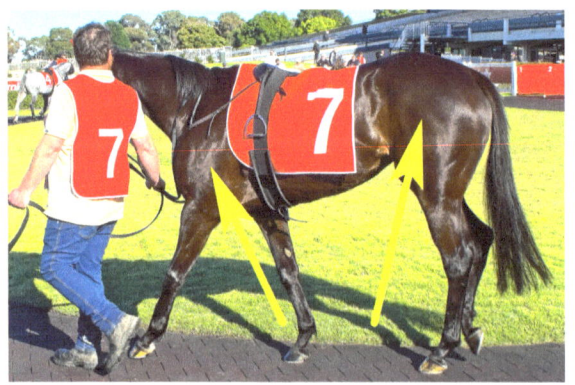

Horse #7 was assessed as Average fitness, as both the shoulder and rear end muscle definition markers weren't strongly apparent, and those regions were somewhat still blank. (Yellow Arrows). She was the perfect example of a horse coming along very nicely but maybe in need of this race. She was very compliant throughout the parade with the only negative being Bit Grinding.

Chapter 24. "Parade Transcripts"

Horse #8   Odds $5.50

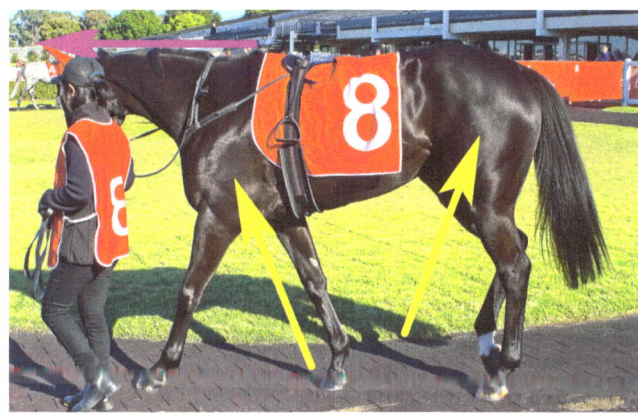

Horse #8 is basically a replica of what I thought about the previous horse, Horse #7. I marked it as Average grade fitness due to the plain shoulder and hindquarter muscle definitions (Yellow Arrows) and viewed it as coming along nicely but needing the run to top off its fitness.

She was also very healthy in the coat, well behaved and had a horizontal neck carriage. (Pink Arrow).

Results -   Winner - Horse 7   Second - Horse 8   Third - Horse 5

Chapter 25. "From Yard to Race"

An important component of a racehorse's success lies in their tractability, or manners, during a race. This chapter explores the notion that there may be correlations between factors recorded in the mounting yard and traits displayed during the race. Can the punter attain some predictability or likelihood as to what one's selections race behaviour may be. Is it likely to travel generously? Will it miss the start? With so much importance placed on Speed Mapping and what position a horse can acquire in the race shape, any information that can be factored in is invaluable for the integrity of the map.

Knowledge of a horse's previous set of pre-race variables and how it responded in the race is additionally invaluable information. I've often noticed horses that seem to perform tractably only when they parade with certain attributes. An example is a horse that parades with an elevated neck for a couple of runs, performing ungenerously by over racing and then presents with a horizontal neck carriage and runs an improved race, travelling sweetly for the rider. I have encountered this many times and occurs with numerous factors. The jig jogger turned relaxed walker, the tail swisher that over races but becomes compliant when the swishing ceases. Record keepers who use comparisons from yard to race will have seen many instances of this. It's a definite advantage knowing what the likelihood is that a horse will perform to its optimum race behaviour from its mounting yard variables.

In Table 17 I've looked at 100 instances of some select yard variables to see how they correlate to 8 race factors or behaviours that are commonly seen during a race. Descriptions of those race variables are as follows.

Easy Loader - This refers to the horse's attitude to entering the barrier. Barrier loading is relevant as it goes to the horse's state of mind. The calmness of an easy loader and the confrontational attitude of the obstinate loader. Criteria for the factor was basically that it walked straight in.
Difficult Loader - This is when the horse shows genuine resistance to going in. Refusal to move forward, using the common escape clause of turning side on and requiring pushing and urging from the attendants. Horses that required some minimal encouragement to go in, but weren't really a problem, weren't recorded in either loading category.
Slow Away - This is when the horse clearly missed the start, losing a length or so to the field.
Over Racing - This occurs in the early stage of the race, prior to the field settling, when a horse throws its head about, refusing to settle and proving difficult for the rider to control.
Travel - This is the term used for a horse that settles well, is very generous to the rider and comfortable with the race pace and field position.
Pulling - This is when the field has settled into a pace, but the horse is wanting to go faster, causing the rider's legs to point forward for leverage, while pulling hard on the reins to restrain the animal.
Extend Late - This is at the end of the race, noting if the horse kept stretching out, as honestly as possible, to the finish line.
Fade - This is the opposite of the late extend. The horse drops back through the field, neck elevated, or head turned, wobbling with tiredness and yielding to the effort.

Table 17 – From Yard to Race Variables

(The count for each variable was 100, so the figures in the table are percentages. Averages for each category are in the last row.)

IV	Factor	Easy Load	Difficult Load	Slow Away	Over Race	Travel	Pull	Extend Late	Fade
Pos	Ears Pricked	53	12	3	4	61	3	21	24
Neg	Ears Negative	38	17	6	4	48	7	25	29

Chapter 25. "From Yard to Race"

IV	Factor	Easy Load	Difficult Load	Slow Away	Over Race	Travel	Pull	Extend Late	Fade
Pos	Bit Play	44	9	5	6	55	5	31	34
Neg	Salivate Mild	41	6	9	5	53	5	36	41
Pos	Still Mouth	62	7	3	2	71	1	63	23
Neg	Head Toss	30	14	23	10	51	9	30	58
Pos	Neck Arched	39	9	8	3	65	3	42	33
Pos	Neck Twisted	37	3	8	2	59	2	38	39
Pos	Neck Horizontal	44	8	5	3	43	4	29	44
Pos	Ground Licker	52	7	11	4	68	2	61	22
Neg	Tension Line	29	16	3	6	51	2	33	51
Neg	Tail Swishing	31	13	10	7	55	7	40	33
Pos	Fit	37	7	4	4	66	4	58	36
Neg	Average	45	11	8	4	53	3	45	48
Neg	Fat	34	5	5	2	50	1	29	66
Neg	Thin	38	9	9	5	59	3	36	61
Pos	Power Walk	53	9	6	1	76	1	73	14
Neg	Walking Short	35	15	12	6	58	2	36	36
Neg	Jig Jogging	29	17	7	8	47	6	37	53
Pos	Double Tracking	40	12	7	2	49	2	41	44
Pos	Focus/Transition	41	3	3	1	62	2	60	22
Neg	Behaviour Negative	30	13	9	5	53	5	43	39
Neg	Bum Sweat	37	8	8	4	65	3	37	38
Neg	Body Sweat	33	14	8	6	48	6	29	46
Pos	Canter Off Positive	46	7	6	1	79	1	74	25
Neg	Canter Off Negative	28	17	5	7	52	3	33	60
26	AVERAGE	39.5	10.3	7.3	4.3	57.6	3.5	41.5	39.2

Using the overall Impact Values from Table 1 and dividing the yard factors into positives and negatives (ie. greater or less than one, Column 1 Table 17) and then comparing them to the averages of the eight race factors, enables an insight into the relationship of the 26 yard factors and the 8 race variables. 12 yard factors were positive and 14 negative and of the race variables, 3 are positive and 5 negatives.

Easy Load – Of the 12 positive yard variables, 10 returned figures over the average and only 2 of the 14 negatives were above average. The highest figures came from Still Mouth, Ears Pricked, Ground Licker, Power Walker and Canter Off Positive. Probably all factors one would expect to be the profile of an easy loader.

Difficult Load – In this negative race factor, 4 of the 12 positive yard factors were above average and 11 of the 14 negatives were over the average. No surprises from the factor profiling of the difficult loaders either, with Ears Negative, Head Toss, Tension Line, Tail Swishing, Walking Short, Jig Jogging, Body Sweat and Canter Off Negative to the fore.

Slow Away – Of the positive yard variables, 3 returned figures above the average, while 9 of the 14 negatives went over the average. Notably here, the head tosser nearly doubled the percentage of the second highest, the short walker. There is a 23% chance that a head tosser will miss the start, and the short walker

Chapter 25. "From Yard to Race"

may be hinting at a reluctance to stride out.

Over Race – Only one of the positive yard factors exceeded the average, whilst 10 of the negatives did. Once again, the head tosser was in the limelight, followed by the jig jogger and tail swisher, all signs of a nervous, apprehensive horse in the yard, that would invoke concern about its race tractability.

Travel – The results for this race variable fall the way one would expect, with 9 of the 12 positive yard factors above average and 3 from 14 of the negatives.

Pulling – This negative race factor returned 3 positive and 7 negative yard factors over the average. Once again, the head tosser, jig jogger and the tail swisher managed the highest figures.

Extend Late – The best figures returned for the late extenders were from those that showed in the yard a possible preparedness to stride out with a good breathing pattern. They were the Still Mouth, Power Walker, Ground Licker and Canter Off Positive. 8 of the 12 positive factors were over the average with only 2 of the 14 negatives achieving above average results.

Fade – 2 of 12 positives and 10 of 14 negative yard factors were above average faders. Prominence naturally included the unfit categories, with the head tosser featuring again.

In taking an overall view of the table, it is probably not unexpected how the yard variables contributed towards the figures of the race variables. With the negative yard factors comprising the makeup of the negative race factors and the positive yard factors the main contributor to the positive race factor results. The whole exercise seems to point to the situation of what one sees in the parade ring, is what one may get in the race, which leads to partially answering why yard factors are positive and negative. Head tossers are often slowly away, don't always travel well and often fade, while power walkers and still mouths are more likely to travel and extend, to example a couple. Working backwards, race performance and habits, can be traced back to parade ring traits.

The relevance and importance of looking at "yard to race" variables, is that they can impact on one of the most vital segments of race analysis, and that is the Speed Map. Mapping has become the first thing many form analysts prepare in their race examination procedure and having all available inputs to formulate a map and being able to adjust it, is paramount.

An example from the table is the Head Toss variable. If a speed mapper was to attend the parade ring and notice a horse head tossing and that horse is pivotal to how the map may work out, then the necessary adjustments can be made for the 23% chance the head tosser may be tardy at the start. Similarly, with all the other positive and negative factors, behavioural based tweaks to the speed map could be applied after viewing horses in the parade ring. The game is about prediction and anything that may help predictive accuracy is worth being aware of.

An additional purpose of looking at "yard to race" correlations is their use in the practice of "In Running" betting via an exchange. The ability to target a horse that may possibly display a race variable, can be very beneficial to an in-run player. Using the head tosser example again, knowing there is a one in four or five chance of them missing the start, anticipating that happening and capitalising on it, through the odds changes, can be very rewarding. There's more on this in an upcoming chapter on betting in the run.

Chapter 26. "From The TV"

Within the wagering world, regular racegoers would definitely be in the minority, as not everyone has the means to regularly attend race meetings. Many punters may not even bet in their local racing jurisdictions, concentrating further afield. The regular attendees would have a distinct advantage when it comes to paddock watching, but there are options for the off-course punter through their race vision provider.

I have done paddock assessments for clients from many different live feed options. Aside from the local options I have access to, they range from a Facebook feed of Mauritius racing to YouTube feeds of Canadian and American racing where they provide fixed camera viewing of the saddling and pre-parade areas.

The only truly reliable and consistent yard vision sources I've encountered are the feeds from Hong Kong and Japan racing. Hong Kong has a very good yard analyst, and they treat the parade as a major part of their production, showing all the horses prior to the jockeys mounting. They use voiceover instead of showing talking heads, allowing their vision to focus on the horses, providing the viewer with ample time to assess them.

Yard watching from the TV does come with its limitations, but it can be a very useful tool, depending on the punter's requirements regarding what and how much they want to see. If it's just to check on their preferred choice, then that's normally always possible. A comprehensive appraisal of the horse? Not always possible. A full field appraisal? Touch and go from my experience, bar Hong Kong and Japan. Other vision, that I haven't encountered, may well be available in other racing jurisdictions and be of the Hong Kong standard, enabling comprehensive yard assessments.

Here are some of the challenges I've experienced when working off the TV.

Vision quality. The horse is in a shadow reducing visibility of coat condition and muscle definitions. The angle of the shot being overhead, head on or too distant, inhibiting full vision of the horse.

Incomplete vision. Not every horse shown, or only shown a rear view of their backsides heading off to the barriers.

Missed variables. Not the fault of the feed provider, as some factors may be exhibited when the horse is out of shot. A horse may jig jog or head toss consistently but cease at the time it was in shot. Purely coincidental. Personally, I've filmed many parades with a 360-degree camera and been surprised with what I've missed when reviewing the footage later. This innovation, of 360-degree camera use, was recently tried by one of my local race clubs and I thought it had great merit for the off-track viewer, providing the ability to scroll the footage and view any horse.

One of the main difficulties when assessing off the TV has been the fitness category. Trying to clearly observe all the components that go into the categories of Fit, Fat, Average and Thin, has over the journey proved unreliable for me. Sure, a big belly or overly thin horse can be easily noted, but when it comes to muscle definition and bulk, determining a fitness category off the TV comes with less decisiveness for me. Sometimes it's clearly visible and a confident fitness judgement can be made, but over the long term, watching from the vision has diminished my accuracy in nailing fitness categories. Due to this, for beginners especially, it may be better to dispense with fitness category gradings off the TV, unless obvious and build a pre-race profile off walks, behaviours and sweats.

How comprehensive one's parade assessments can be, is reliant on the vision available and it would clearly be a reduced analysis compared to the on-course observer. However, not all is lost, and many beneficial factors can be used from the vision.

Chapter 26. "From The TV"

The following is a list of variables one should be able to pick up consistently off the TV feed, given reasonable vision quality.

Facial Expressions	Tension Line
Ears Pricked	Tail Swishing
Ears Negative	Tail Jammed
Bit Play	Power Walk
Salivate Mild	Walking Short
Salivate Heavy	Jig Jogging
Still Mouth	Double Tracking
Head Toss	Behaviour Negative
Neck Arched	Bum Sweat
Neck Twisted	Body Sweat
Neck Horizontal	Ground Licker

On this list are the variables that might prove difficult to determine consistently.

Underbelly Negative	Droppings Loose
Hip Pointing	Droppings Firm
Glowing Coat	Groom Negative
Dappled Coat	Canter Off Positive
Dull Coat	Canter Off Negative
Size Big	Rump Top Pos. or Neg.
Size Small	Money Mark Pos. or Neg.
Neck Pos. or Neg.	Shoulder Positive
Rib Cage Pos. or Neg.	Flanks Negative
Racing Dimple Pos. or Neg.	Thigh Negative
Focus/Transition	

Looking at the second list, my experience is that getting a shot good enough to make a judgement on the variable consistently, is often hit and miss. At times there is no problem and factors such as a negative underbelly or a pointing hip can be clearly seen. The same for many of the factors that compile into the fitness gradings such as, the Money Mark, Rib Cage, Racing Dimple, Flanks, Shoulder, Thigh, Neck condition and Rump Top. Sometimes what you see with these factors allows for a confident Fit, Fat, Average or Thin fitness marking, but having filmed hundreds of paddock parades, I've found that a lot of horses that I've categorised as Fit on course, wouldn't qualify for that grade off the footage and vice versa. So, tread a little warily with fitness decisions off the TV.

Marking coats off the vision can be inconsistent too. I mark a glowing coat when it is a real standout compared to the rest of the field, as generally the bulk of the horses will have some degree of sheen to their coats and determining this off the vision is less accurate. With dapples, dull coats and coat richness, I often here these conditions mentioned by the media yard analysts and sometimes I can see them on the TV and often not. As for marking droppings, it's obvious that it needs to be caught in the action, on screen, to determine which horse to mark it for. Size, big or small, may be possible to mark if a good distant shot is available, where there are multiple horses on screen that can be gauged for any obvious differences in size. Unfortunately, with the canter off factors, the vision has usually turned to interviews on the channel I mainly watch, so marking those factors is rarely available off the TV for me.

Turning to the first list, a lot of the variables here are easily identifiable off the TV. Even if the vision of the horse was completely black and just a silhouette, looking at the outlines of variables such as, neck carriages, walks, ear positions, tail positions and head tosses, they are all easily discernible and marking those factors efficiently shouldn't be a problem. Mouth salivations and bum sweats are noticeable because of their white colour, while body sweats on the neck, flanks and elsewhere are generally easily spotted given a reasonable

Chapter 26. "From The TV"

picture. Bit Play, Still Mouth and Facial Expressions may require a closer shot but can be identified most times.

Even though horse watching off the TV does come with some challenges, I still believe that enough can be gleaned to make it imperative, that if one has vision access, they should at the minimum, use it to check on the horse or horses they intend to bet on. Many times, people have asked me post-race how a beaten horse looked in the parade and I've told them it couldn't be supported off how it paraded. So, a reasonable handle on factor identification and a check of the parade via the vision, should be in my opinion, a basic procedure for punters prior to betting.

Chapter 27. "In Running" Horse Watching Thoughts

"This section may be more applicable to those that have access to a betting exchange that allows back and lay wagering during a race, although some of the in-race factors looked at may be helpful to video race replay watchers."

Betting in the run has become popular and competitive in Australia, with turnover during races in the many thousands. It has created a new breed of very sharp punters, all with their own strategies and angles, attending tracks, taking up their preferred positions with their laptops and game plans. In the UK it appears to be at a whole different level, an extremely competitive market, with the use of drones supplying live vision and now the home-based players can access advanced software that receives live data from timing equipment positioned around the racecourse.

Success can be very dependent on the medium used to watch the race, as each one differs in their timing of delivery to the end user. Obviously being on track and watching live, or off live monitors, provides the best medium, but I am aware of successful operators here in Australia who use analogue radio as their race source, which comes in at around a two second delay. From what I've witnessed, they know the race callers' idiosyncrasies so well that they can anticipate what's happening through the tone of the caller's voice. The biggest vision delays come from TV and internet feeds, which I've read can be between three and ten seconds.

Being on track with the quickest live feed doesn't guarantee success, as it is an extremely cutthroat game, with competition from other slick operators and wildly fluctuating markets that are compiled of trade out bets from off course players, radio players bets and off course vision players bets and more. However, I have dabbled successfully in in-running betting and have benefitted from being on course. One of the advantages I've noticed centres around the race callers and their requirement to call horse positions down through the field. Quite often when horses are approaching the home turn, pressure has mounted, horses are making moves both forward and backwards at the head of the field, riders are pulling their mounts out to make runs, but the caller is still working through his call to the rear of the field. This delay in front end information being called is where the on-track bettor can jump in and utilise their advantage over the other, "on delay" players.

From my experience, I quickly realised that it was imperative that a clearly defined strategy or plan, as to what you were going to do or look for in a race, was required going in. Simply trying to wait until you thought you could pick the winner emerging in the home straight, didn't cut it for me. By the time that occurred, all the sharpies had been and gone, the odds were gone with them, and I was getting very little matched and usually at short odds. My first plan of attack or strategy was to sit in a position close to the winning post and only bet when I was sure I knew the winner, with the idea that I would just take all the trade out bets and scraps available and hope for some close finishes, where I could identify the winner and capitalise on all the money that got it wrong. This proved worthwhile. Another strategy I employed was the "win/lose turning point" method, as I tagged it. This involved the targeting of a single horse, short in the market and usually one from the parade ring that I wasn't keen on. The idea behind it being that every horse in a race can be observed reaching a point where they are likely to either win or lose and this was the time to pounce with either a back or lay bet, depending on the direction I could determine the result going. Having to focus on only one horse was a lot easier than trying to scan across the field continually to see what was happening, and this enabled me to be sharper and quicker with my bets, something I wasn't very good at compared to other players I associated with.

Just as horses display traits in the parade ring, they can also display traits or actions in a race and so give the in-run bettor an opportunity to identify them and benefit off them. Table 18 shows the results from an 800-race analysis of horse factors commonly seen within a race. There are five negative variables that may constitute a lay bet and two positive factors that may lean towards a back bet.

Chapter 27. "In Running" Horse Watching Thoughts

Slow Away. The horse missed the jump from the starting gates by around a length or more.

Head Toss. This is where the horse won't settle comfortably on the bit and throws its head up in the air and shakes it about. Usually occurs early in the race when field positions have been taken up and most horses have settled.

Mouth Open. The horse races with its mouth open. Can be clearly seen off race vision.

Pulling. This is when the horse refuses to settle, over races and the jockey's legs are usually pointing forward and they are having difficulty restraining them.

Head Dip. This is generally one of the first signs a horse has had enough. The horse departs from its normal head carriage, putting in a big dip for a stride. It usually reoccurs and the horse begins to fade. Very noticeable on leaders.

Travelling. This is a positive where the horse comfortably travels on the bit for the rider, no pulling or reefing. Forehead angle is close to the vertical and the jockey's hands sit quietly on the horse's neck. Like the canter off position described in the yard variables chapter.

Jock's Elbows. This refers to the pumping of the jockeys' elbows when encouraging the horse. The factor was marked identifying the last jockey to start pumping their mount. Basically a "last one off the leash" variable. Mostly marked when the pressure goes on in the race, turning for home.

Table 18 – "In Running" Variables

Prices used were the official Starting Prices, not Betfair exchange prices.
The < $8 bracket was used as horses more in the market are more likely to get matched.

800 Races	Slow Away	Head Toss	Mouth Open	Pulling	Head Dip	Travelling	Jock's Elbows
Count	236	264	560	124	128	76	164
Winners	8	24	40	12	2	36	104
Win %	3.4	9.1	7.1	9.7	.78	47.3	63.4
< $8 Count	60	96	216	52	44	40	100
< $8 Winners	4	20	28	8	1	16	72
< $8 Win %	6.6	20.8	12.9	15.4	2.2	38.1	72

Looking at Table 18 results shows a lot of poor win percentages for the negative variables and strong percentages for the two positive factors, enforcing the possibility, that betting the variables may be a worthwhile angle and that angle may lean more towards the lay side than the back side. It's probable that these figures may be enhanced for betting purposes when married up with parade ring factors. If a horse has displayed negative fitness or behaviour during the parade and then that negativity is compounded by the identification of poor race variables, then that creates a greater surety on an in running bet placement.

One of the problems encountered with betting in the run is getting one's bets matched. With the variables used here, save for maybe the Head Dip and Jock's Elbows, most occur early in a race, when there is a greater chance of getting matched via trade out bets from pre-race punters and at a time when many punters are sitting back waiting for the race to develop. The Slow Away factor would require one to be very slick, as this is one the sharp operators are very alert to. The Jock's Elbows factor can be hit and miss getting matched, as I've tried it plenty of times and it occurs at a time in the race when the action is really happening, but I found it worthwhile, even for one of the slower operators like me.

Chapter 27. "In Running" Horse Watching Thoughts

The "In Running" markets can be very lucrative, and I suspect that the majority of strategies used are based on the "positioning" of the horse in the race. If so, this may imply that the identification of "horse behavioural" factors, like those previously mentioned, may be underutilized in determining a bet during the race. Personally, I found it easier to strike a bet (back or lay) as soon as a "head tosser" was observed, than wait and try and pick the winner from a long way out, in competition with a lot of sharp operators.

Chapter 28. Applying The Knowledge – Data Usage

"A primary use of yard data is to have the final say in whether to bet or not."
Following the assessment of a horse's parade, the question should be asked, do the behavioural and physical opinions of that assessment warrant the signing off on a wager, that our form study has deemed worthy? The knowledge obtained from the parade ring can be the final link in the wagering decision process and a very powerful one at that. Countless times I've witnessed well fancied horses in the markets parade behaviourally poor and physically below optimum.

This is stating the obvious, but to use the data you must first obtain it. Make the effort to get to the mounting yard or watch the vision. This may require a change of habit from some seasoned racegoers, but I can guarantee a whole new world of benefits will surface. My personal belief is that yard assessments can be used effectively as a "stand alone" method for betting on racehorses. No other conventional form factors such as times, barriers, weights etc need be included, save for possibly the public odds close to race time, as they contain most of the form information. I have supplied the data to clients who have been successful wagering in this manner.

Basic Usage

Besides the most common use of the parade analysis being to either reinforce or disregard a wager, the value of some recordkeeping can't be underestimated. There's value in knowing the habits of a horse from some of its previous outings and great value in being able to monitor the accuracy and improvement in one's own yard assessments. I found it very rewarding reviewing my analysis for a meeting after the results were known. The recordkeeping may only entail scribbling some notes in the racebook or a notepad or may be the entering of the details into a spreadsheet, as was my preferred method. My program automatically converted the factors into a value, then a rating and then an odds line and saved everything to a database page. The setup was probably more comprehensive than most would require but any form of recordkeeping is worthwhile.

Over time the yard analyst may develop a favourite set of variables, or a particular profile of a horse they require to see, before having a bet. Experience tells them they are better off waiting for a horse that fits their criteria. I myself seem to be subscribing to this more often, with a stronger vigilance towards identifying two of my preferred factors, being the Still Mouth and the Canter Off Positive horse. If I had to try and live off two factors it would be those two. On the flip side, I could never back a Jig Jogging, Head Tossing, Body Sweater.

The level of use of yard data basically comes down to how much the yard watcher wants to put into it. If that means a brief viewing, at the parade ring or off the TV, to check on their preferred selection, then that's fine. It will help long term. Same at the other end of the spectrum, with the collection of data points through spreadsheeting and a database.

Ratings

A form of race analysis that is very popular is the creation of a rating for each horse in a race. These can be based on differing areas of past performance, such as a Speed Rating, or a Class and Weight rating and a pre-race parade rating can also be calculated. As long as there is a data point value then a rating calculation is possible, and in turn, an odds line can be constructed.

For each factor assigned to a horse in the parade ring, we can draw on the metrics from the Impact Value Table or the A/E Index Table to compile the rating. Simply multiply the values together for the final rating figure. As I've mentioned previously, the tables are based on my identification of the variables, but if a reasonable amount of competence has been achieved in factor identification, I'm sure use of the tables would produce a very reasonable rating.

Alternatively, you may prefer to score a horse out of say, 100 or 50, based on the overall variables seen in the horse's parade, rather than recording and tallying the values of each individual factor. Make an overall judgement of the horse and allocate a number for it.

Below is an actual race that was supplied to a client, using the A/E Index tables for the metrics.

No.	Odds	Factors.	Values	Rating	My Odds
1.	28	Facial Exp, Bit Play, Neck Arch Ears Neg, Fat	.81 .94 .97 .81 .64	.38	42.2
2.	2.1	Bit Play, Power Walk, Fit	.94 .96 .92	.83	3.30
3.	13	Bit Play, Fit, Jig Jog	.94 .92 .75	.65	8
4.	200	Bit Play, Thin, Head Toss Tension Line	.94 .64 .73 .77	.34	56.2
5.	36	Bit Play, Jig Jog, Average	.94 .75 .79	.56	13.2
6.	270	Fat, Walking Short	.64 .74	.47	23
7.	38	Tension Line, Facial Exp, Head Toss Drop Firm, Fat	.77 .81 .73 .85 .64	.25	112
8.	11	Bit Play, Fat, Behaviour Neg	.94 .64 .74	.45	26.2
9.	190	Hip Point, Bit Play, Thin	.71 .94 .64	.43	29.9
10.	4.5	Bit Play, Fit, Salivate Mild	.94 .92 .97	.84	3.20
11.	20	Ears Neg, Average, Head Toss Behaviour Neg, Body Sweat	.81 .79 .73 .74 .89	.31	70.3

The race is a good example of how using either the Impact Values, or the A/E Index metrics, can produce a solid rating and odds market. The market is a good representation of how I felt the visual was when doing the yard. It basically narrowed down to a two horse go, with a larger gap back to some secondary chances, with horse number 2 being successful. This format of ratings, percentages and odds is how I supplied the parade ring information to clients, as they were usually figure orientated and weren't really concerned with what the variables from the yard were. That was my domain, and they were more interested in finding value amongst the figures.

Machine Learning - Artificial Intelligence (AI)

Neural Networks, Naïve Bayes, Gradient Boosting, Logistic Regression!!....... Those titles have likely been enough to make you skip to the next section, but stick around, things are becoming very user friendly in this area. AI is heavily upon us, entrenched in all aspects of our lives and as it seems with a lot of these innovations, that appear beyond most people's comprehension, they eventually come down to a level of useability. That is the scenario with Machine Learning, AI and Data Modelling techniques and the punter that keeps or has access to data, hasn't been left out. If you have a laptop or computer and can handle a spreadsheet then you are good to go. There is very good software available, aimed at the average punter, written by a punting data scientist, regularly updated and simple to use. I've been using it for quite a while, and it is surprising the level of analysis achievable. **MySportsAI** from **smartersig.com.**
I've noticed an increasing amount of racing database suppliers, tipsters and rating services offering AI based information, such as, "Neural Ratings" and "AI Selections". It's an area that will continue to grow and develop and should be embraced by punters as an analysis tool for their data.

My Data Usage Journey

Describing how my horse watching practices evolved may be helpful for those starting out to possibly fast

Chapter 28. Applying The Knowledge – Data Usage

track their own journey in achieving factor identification proficiency.

For a long time, I would attend the mounting yards, peruse the horses and decide on which one I liked, never recording any notes and using basic factors, such as glowing coat, to arrive at my decision. Looking back my selections would be best described as a "hunch". I began to realise that there was a myriad of things that could be inspected on the parading horse. From the creases the muscles made all over the horse, to their walks, behaviours and bodily functions such as sweats, saliva and droppings. Then came the realisation that these things were measurable and could be differentiated between. The state of the muscle definitions could explain the stage of fitness, types of walks could explain a horse's physical feeling and provide an insight into the mental state along with the negative attributes such as nervous sweating.

From that point on I began to keep notes of what I was observing. Very basic and easy to do, just symbols or initials of the factor alongside the horse's name in the racebook. The recording of a horse's neck carriage is a good example. This was just a line drawn of the angle of the neck, assuming the horse was walking to the right. So, a line angled diagonally up to the right meant the horse was carrying its head high and diagonally down depicted a ground licker with the horizontals and other angles in between. I ended up with boxes full of racebooks filled with these markings.

Part of the fascination with doing all this was going through the racebook at the end of the day and matching neck angles to finishing positions and market odds. It was interesting to see how each neck angle would start to grade itself, performance wise, over time and how that grading often reflected the inaccuracies of the market odds. Same scenario applied to other factors too. Eventually this data recording method succumbed to the natural progression of using a laptop and spreadsheet on track. Even so I would still advocate using this method to expedite one's yard analysis proficiency.

Unless you feel competent, initially it may be best to dispense with fitness judgements and select a couple of factors to concentrate on. My suggestion would be neck factors and a group of negatives like, head toss, tension line, tail swishing, jig jogging, body sweaters and bad behaviours. All that is required to be marked in the racebook or form sheet is a line corresponding to the neck angle and an X to denote any of the negatives. Simple to do, achievable off the TV vision and when the markings are compared over time against performance, and the market, I'm sure you will begin to see the value in identifying pre-race horse factors and gain a confidence boost in your ability to mark them.

Chapter 29. "Final Thoughts"

In this final chapter I will reiterate and reinforce some important points and offer some advice for those that have familiarised themselves with the variables and their values and are ready to begin doing yard analysis. Remember, if you have the will to learn horse watching techniques, you will succeed at it. There is no prerequisite for horse knowledge needed.

- Approach the yard as being a "blank canvas". Shed all form knowledge, biases, influences and preconceived ideas. Be clinical in marking what you see.

- Don't force things. Sometimes nothing comes to you. Hundreds of times I've left the yard thinking the parade was "all over the shop". Nothing definitive eventuated and therefore the race may best be left alone.

- Remember, the positive and negative aspects of the variables are not my opinions or those of experienced horse people, they are from the collected data.

- Don't hesitate to write notes/symbols on the variables you see. Reviewing horses' performances against your markings is a worthwhile and revealing exercise.

- Familiarise yourself with the workflows of Chart 1 – Factor Groupings. Especially the variables used to evaluate the fitness categories of, Fit, Fat, Average and Thin.

- Understand the metrics used. Impact Values and Actual/Expected Index. Below 1 is a negative, around 1 is normal and above 1 is a positive.

- Also understand how the metrics are dynamic and respond when influenced by race distance, market position and when in combination with fitness categories.

- Perusal of the Impact Values and A/Es would suggest that a huge aspect to this horse watching caper comes down to the disposition of the animal in the race day parade. Fortunately, the variables that lead to the evaluation of a racehorse's disposition are more easily identifiable to the watcher who is just starting out. Hence, it may be wise to concentrate on the "Walks", "Behavioural" and "Others" categories as depicted in Chart 1 – Factor Groupings. My experience tells me that the grading of factors in the "Physical Structures" list and in turn the "Fitness" category proves to be the most difficult for beginners, whereas the other categories seem to be more straightforward to identify. Save for big underbellies and thin, angular rear ends, which should be more readily noticeable, let the other fitness variables come to you over time as you assess more parades. Which they will. The other groups will still produce a very powerful insight into race performance predictions.

- Concentrate on variables that you feel you can comfortably identify and build horse profiles from. Positive and negative. You may find a group of more easily identifiable factors such as, bit chewing, tail swishing, jig jogging and head tossing represents a profile that implicates an apprehensive, nervous horse and an undesirable disposition to wager on. Whereas a calm walker with a horizontal neck carriage, static mouth and glowing coat is a profile that qualifies as a potential bet. It doesn't take long to be able to recognise the style of horse you prefer to see in a parade.

Most of all, never forget the privilege of being in the presence of such magnificent animals.
And remember,
"It's not really winnings unless you spend it. Just account balance movement".
"Make a decision to never ever "Hunch Punt" again. Have a data point, a form factor, a reason"
"Knowledge is studying to find the best rated horse. Wisdom is knowing if the odds are value"

Chapter 29. "Final Thoughts"

"My Journey"

With a strong family interest in racing and horses, where my father was a serious punter and racehorse owner and my late brother was a jockey, it was odds on that I would be influenced too. And I was. From the very first meeting attended I was fascinated by the appearance of the horses and over forty years later that passion continues with the challenge of pre-race assessment and the enjoyment of "staring at horses".

Apart from the horse watching experience I've also enjoyed the "hands on" experience along the journey, having owned, broken in, retrained, rehabilitated, shod, ridden trackwork and at one stage obtaining a licence and training a few winners.

The yard analysis side began with providing my thoughts to my father, which led to supplying them to a bookmaker and then on to an interstate professional punter. In 2007 I was recruited to a large racing data collection and investment operation under the title of "Equine Condition Analyst" and became a foundation member of their research and development program into pre-race horse analysis. My assignment there was to specialise in fitness assessments. In this position I attended up to six meetings a week for over a decade and this frequency on Victorian racetracks had me referred to as "Zeljko Steve" by some of the regulars. During my time with the company, I was also involved in staff training, both on course and at seminars, which I found very rewarding.

After moving on from that operation I supplied yard information to punters and groups based in Asia and Australia and was a keen collector of data via the on-course presence and recorded vision and that data forms the backbone of this book. I've also been lucky enough to travel and have supplied clients with yard assessments from Japan, South Korea, Singapore, Hong Kong, America and all Australian states. I'm still feeding the passion by attending races, collecting data, photographing everything, still learning new angles and trying to refine the "edge".

Steve Lang